SILVER MARKS
OF THE WORLD

HAMLYN
London New York Sydney Toronto

SILVER MARKS OF THE WORLD

JAN DIVIŠ

HAMLYN
London · New York · Sydney · Toronto

Illustrations by
Jaromír Knotek
Translated by
Joy Moss-Kohoutová
Graphic design by Aleš Krejča
© Copyright Artia, Prague
1976
Designed and produced by
Artia for The Hamlyn
Publishing Group Limited
London·New York·Sydney
Toronto
Astronaut House, Feltham,
Middlesex, England
First published 1976
Reprinted 1978

ISBN 0 600 38156 0
Printed in Czechoslovakia
by TSNP Martin
2/10/04/51-03

CONTENTS

INTRODUCTION

Hallmarks stamped on silver items are intended to protect the buyer. They guarantee that the content of the precious metal in every individual piece corresponds to legal requirements. However, for us today the hallmarks on antique silver pieces are also invaluable aids in determining the place and date they were produced, which is the most important and most necessary information. This book is intended as a guide to the most important of these marks and a practical and ready source of information to the amateur and specialist alike — in fact to everyone who, for love of it or in the line of duty, comes into contact with "the Queen of Metals".

This handbook has therefore been compiled according to these practical considerations and starts from what the observer sees: the arrangement of the marks — based on the subjects they depict — enables the reader speedily and easily to make his way around in the book, and the text concerning the drawings of the individual marks tells him about the town and country where the hallmark was used, the date when it was employed and, if possible, the purity which the mark guarantees. The marks are arranged according to the following pattern: letters in alphabetical order (1—669), numerals (670—695), human figures (696—887), mammals (888—1140), birds (1141—1302), other animals (1303—1359), plants (1360—1482), heavenly bodies (1483—1517), architecture (1518—1591), objects (1592—1816), emblems (1817—1994).

Regarding the origin and age of the items, the most reliable answer is provided by marks stamped by control bodies, whether these were municipalities, state institutions or guilds. These marks have been incorporated in this book to the fullest extent of present-day knowledge. Furthermore, those marks which are unusually important in determining the country and place of origin of the item have been included, such as a special duty mark, or the assignee's hallmark. The other hallmarks (maker's marks, date letters, special marks for purity, etc.) had to be omitted because they would have gone beyond the bounds of this volume. However, an elementary choice of marks of silversmiths working in the U.S.A. has been included because in the United States there was no state or other control of purity standards and so the hallmarks of American producers are the only indication determining items of American provenance.

The origin and development of marking differed in individual countries and states of the world. This is explained in the brief outline of marking and hallmark regulations which follows, presented by countries and states whose marks are included in this book and whose silver products deserve attention. If the name of a goldsmith appears in the book it should be remembered that in most countries the goldsmith made items of both gold and silver; a goldsmith was anyone who worked with precious metals, and, in most cases, not even official decrees distinguished between a goldsmith and a silversmith.

It is hoped that this book will be of help chiefly to lovers of antique silver and, therefore, the main stress is on hallmarks used in the past. For this reason the most recent date for the choice of marks is the period between the world wars, i. e. the 1930s.

Prague, November 1974   Jan Diviš

HALLMARKING
IN INDIVIDUAL STATES

AUSTRALIA

No official marks exist in Australia for items made of precious metals since most of the silver pieces are imported from England.

In 1923 producers attempted to introduce marks for several Australian areas. These marks, however, provided no official guarantees and are no longer used.

AUSTRIA

1366 — a decree of the Austrian Princes Albrecht and Leopold was issued on assaying precious metals. Two guild masters were named to test the purity, both being under the supervision of the master of the mint.

1659 — a patent of Emperor Leopold I permitted work in 14 lot silver.

1708 — a patent of Emperor Joseph I permitted a purity of 13 lots and 14 lots (known as the Augsburger und Wiener-Probe).

1737 — a patent of Emperor Charles VI introduced a purity standard of 15 lots.

1774 — a patent of Empress Maria Theresa depicted for the first time the hallmarks that had to be used.

1784 — beginning with this year, state control of purity commenced in Austria — but only in Vienna.

1786 — state control of purity was introduced in Galicia (see Poland).

1806 — a uniform state system of marking throughout the entire Austro-Hungarian Empire was introduced, except for Hungary, Slovakia (under Hungarian domination), and Transylvania.

1866 — from 1 August new hallmarks and marks of purity for silver, calculated in thousandths instead of the previous lot system, became valid. These hallmarks are now used in Hungary as well. Permitted purity standards are 950, 900, 800 and 750/1000.

1872 — the marks in use were altered so that the letter indicating the seat of the assay office became part of the purity mark. These marks were used in the Austrian Republic until 1921, in Czechoslovakia until 1922, in part of Poland until 1920, in part of Yugoslavia until 1919, and in Hungary until 1937.

1921 — marks of the new Austrian Republic came into force with the law of 21 October.

Bibliography:

Knies, K.: Die Punzirung in Österreich. Vienna 1896.

Reitzner, V.: Alt-Wien-Lexikon für Österreichische u. Süddeutsche Kunst u. Kunstgewerbe. Band III.: Edelmetalle u. deren Punzen. Vienna 1952.

BELGIUM

1484 — Maximilian issued a decree for his Flanders territories evidently affecting the use of date letters.

1501 — Archduke Philip the Handsome, as Governor of the Netherlands, issued regulations for goldsmiths in Holland, Seeland, and Friesland and on 2 February, 1502, for Antwerp, and probably for other towns as well.
Hallmarked items: 1. town emblem under the crown; 2. date letter; 3. maker's mark.

1551 — in Brussels Emperor Charles V issued goldsmiths' regulations for the Netherlands which also applied to part of northern France (Artois), today's Belgium (except for the principality of Liège), the Grand Duchy of Luxemburg and the Kingdom of the Netherlands.

1556 — the Netherlands came under the Spanish line of the Habsburgs. The existing system of hallmarking remained in force.

1612 — Governor Albrecht issued a decree ordering the introduction of another hallmark, in addition to the town mark already in use.
A specimen of hallmarking from this time:

a, b) Ypres town marks; c) date letter 1684/85; d) maker's mark (P. Vost).

1797 — Austria's Netherlands came under French rule. French rulings of 1797 (19th Brumaire Year VI) now became valid.

1815—30 — Belgium formed part of the Kingdom of the Netherlands, but marks other than those used in the Netherlands were used on Belgian territory.

1831 — following the establishment of the Kingdom of Belgium a new ruling was issued on hallmarking, based on the French model. Hallmarking became obligatory.

1869 — the law of 5 June, 1868, came into force, abolishing obligatory state control and permitting any standard of purity. Nevertheless, items with a purity of 800 and 900/1000 could be submitted for assaying and marked. State marks of purity were introduced as well as the personal marks of the assayers. The maker's mark was not required. These marks remained in force until 1 January, 1942.

Bibliography:
Crooÿ L. and F.: Les Poinçons Belges d'Orfèvrerie depuis le XVe s. jusqu'à la Révolution Française. Brussels 1910.

BULGARIA

Nothing is known about the hallmarking of items made of precious metals in Bulgaria in older times. This is evidently the result of the Turkish occupation which lasted from 1393 to 1878 (and in the south of the country until 1881). Hallmarking was probably carried out according to the Turkish system.

1910 — the law of 1 March, 1907, came into force. Items were marked with an official stamp of purity and the maker's mark. Permitted fineness standards were 950, 900, 850, 750 and 500/1000.

Bibliography:

Georgieva, S. — Buchinski, D.: Staroto zlatarstvo v Vratsa. Sofia 1959.

Zontshev, J.: Der Goldschatz von Panagjurischste. 1950.

CANADA

Silversmiths who settled in Canada in the period when it was a French colony (1700—1763) used marks similar to those of French makers: the first letters of the maker's name shown in a shield and over them either a crown or the French fleur de lis or else a star. After 1763, during the period of British rule, the marks of Canadian makers changed. Only the monogram of the maker remained in the shield which was now rectangular or semi-circular. These hallmarks are very similar to the marks of goldsmiths from the Channel Islands and therefore, when it comes to identification, mistakes can easily be made. Goldsmiths in the provinces of Montreal and Quebec added the word MONTREAL or QUEBEC to their marks at this time. The goldsmiths from Halifax (Nova Scotia) similarly added the monogram "H" or "HX", or "XNS". The monograms "StJ" or "NB" were used in St John (New Brunswick). At the beginning of the 19th century Canadian hallmarks imitated English ones.

Examples even occur of imitations of the English official hallmarks, for instance the duty mark. In 1908 a law came into effect — valid until 1946 — requiring a purity of 925/1000 in silver work.

Bibliography:

Langdon, J. E.: Canadian Silversmiths and their Marks. Vermont 1960.

CZECHOSLOVAKIA

1324 — the oldest record of a goldsmiths' brotherhood in Prague.

1562 — Ferdinand I approved the guild rules of Prague goldsmiths. All items weighing more than half a hřivna (a Prague hřivna weighed c. 253 grams; 64 Prague groschen were made from one hřivna) had to be submitted to the guild for testing. The items had to be marked as follows: 1. town mark; 2. maker's mark (mostly monogram).

1776 — new guild regulations for Prague goldsmiths. Provision for the election of three makers to hallmark silver pieces. The Prague goldsmith's guild was the so-called Land Guild, i.e. all goldsmiths in the Kingdom of Bohemia were obliged to observe its regulations. Only 13 lot silver was permitted to be used. A special hallmark was decreed for lower standards of purity.

1785 — 15 lot silver was allowed to be used and a new mark was introduced for it.

1788 — the following purities for silver were stipulated by law: 13 lot (= 812.5/1000) and 15 lot (= 937.5/1000). Hallmarking was still carried out by appointed guild masters. Now, items were marked with three stamps: 1. the maker's mark; 2. the mark of Bohemia (for Prague), or the mark of the town where the maker worked; 3. the mark of purity.

1806 — a basic change occurred in the hereditary Austrian lands in hallmarking precious metals: the right to mark the products was taken from the guilds and given to the state. (For details on this and subsequent changes see Austria.)

1921 — old Austrian marks of 1872 were abolished and Czechoslovak hallmarks were introduced. Permitted purity: 950, 900, 800 and 750/1000.

1929 — introduction of new marks and new purities of 959, 925, 900, 835 and 800/1000. These marks were valid until 1940.

Note: Slovakia, as part of the former Austro-Hungarian Empire, belonged to Hungary until 1918 and was naturally subject to Hungarian regulations.

Bibliography:

Hráský, J.: Značkování výrobků z drahých kovů (In: Pražský sborník historický VIII), Prague 1973.

Schirek, C.: Die Punzierung in Mähren. Brno 1902.

DENMARK

1445 — a royal decree, valid throughout the kingdom, required that every item be stamped with a town hallmark and a maker's mark.

1523 — until this year, Danish regulations were generally valid for Sweden.

1685 — a decree was issued by Christian IV for Copenhagen, which was the model for other towns of the kingdom as well as for larger towns of Norway, introduced basic changes in the system of marking: each object weighing over 5 lots had to be submitted to the master of the mint for assay. The master then marked it with the town emblem, with a mark of the month, and with his own mark. Henceforth there were four marks on an item: 1. the town mark (København); 2. the assayer's mark (master C. Ludolf); 3. the mark of the month (April); 4. the maker's mark.

14

1814 — until this year Danish regulations applied to Norway as well.

1893 — the law of 5 April, 1888, came into force. Items had now to be marked with 1. the producer's mark; 2. the purity figure with the letter "S"; 3. an official mark with date. The lowest permissible purity standard was 826/1000.

Bibliography:

Boje, Ch. A.: Danske Guld og Solf Smedemaeker for 1870. Copenhagen 1951.

Orlik, J.: Danske Guldsmedes Maerker. Copenhagen 1919.

EGYPT

From 1 September, 1916, the hallmarking system established by the law of 8 August, 1906, came into force. Items produced in Egypt were stamped with three marks:

1. purity and assay office (Cairo 800/1000); 2. government mark; 3. date letter.

These three marks were stamped on all the main parts of a product. Small items were only marked with a stamp of quality. The law of 1906 and the marks used were valid until 1946.

ENGLAND

First records of English goldsmiths' guilds date from the 12th century.

1180 — Henry II; establishment of a goldsmiths' guild having the right to use the hallmark with the leopard's head.

1238 — Henry III; introduction of a silver purity assay to avoid fraud.

1300—1544 — Edward I; in this period the hallmark with the leopard's head indicated the Sterling standard of purity of 11 oz 2 dwt (= 925/1000), corresponding to the purity of the coinage instituted in the reign of Henry II (1154—89).

1336 — the goldsmiths' guild issued regulations on hallmarking and introduced the following marks:
1. leopard's head;
2. maker's mark;
3. date letter.

Leopard's head, the hallmark for London, was also used by Exeter and York from the 18th century.

Maker's marks consisted first of symbols, then during the 17th century of letters (generally the initials of the maker's Christian name and surname or of the surnames of a partnership) either alone or with a symbol, a favourite one being a crown or coronet. During the period of the Britannia Standard (1697—1720), however, it was compulsory for the maker's mark to consist of the first two letters of his surname.

Date letter for London was changed every year in May and indicates the age of the piece. When the alphabet was exhausted (twenty letters from A to U were used, excluding J), the shape of the letter and shield was changed. Other towns with assay offices each had their own system.

1423 — introduction of the "mark of origin". Every office had its own mark, for instance London had the leopard's head.

The subsequent development of English hallmarking might seem very complicated, but the whole problem can be explained by using the example of the marking system employed in London (the specimen marks are based on M. Rosenberg).

Until 1544 silver items were stamped with three marks:
1. leopard's head;
2. date letter;
3. maker's mark.

Specimen:

 MAKER'S MARK

In 1544 a fourth mark was added, the "lion passant". The model for this was taken from the royal emblem. It indicated the "Sterling" purity — 11 oz 2 dwt (= 925/1000). As the symbol of Sterling purity it was used in the other towns of England as well. Until 1821 the lion was shown en face, thereafter in profile.

Specimen:

   MAKER'S
MARK

From 1697 to 1720 the required purity was 11 oz 10 dwt (= 958.3/1000), with these hallmarks:
a) figure of Britannia, b) lion's head erased, superseding and replacing marks 1 and 4 (leopard's head and lion passant).

Products of Britannia standard were stamped with four marks as follows: 1. figure of Britannia; 2. lion's head erased; 3. date letter; 4. maker's mark.

Specimen:

   MAKER'S
MARK

Since the silver "Britannia" purity proved too soft for general everyday use, in 1719 an Act was passed enabling silversmiths to return to the normal Sterling standard from 1 June, 1720, so that henceforth both series of hallmarks were used side by side. In 1784 for England and Scotland (but not for Ireland), a duty mark was introduced confirming that a tax had been paid for the purity assay. It showed the head of the ruling king or queen and was used until 1890. Therefore, from 1784 onwards every work of silver had five different marks:

    1. leopard's head; 2. date letter; 3. lion passant;
    4. duty mark; 5. maker's mark.
Specimen:

 MAKER'S
MARK

From 1890, once again four marks were in use, since the
    duty mark was abolished:
A/ For lower purity:
    1. leopard's head; 2. date letter; 3. lion passant;
    4. maker's mark.
Specimen:

 MAKER'S
MARK

B/ For higher purity:
    1. date letter; 2. Britannia; 3. lion's head erased;
    4. maker's mark.
Specimen:

 MAKER'S
MARK

Bibliography:
Bradbury, F.: British and Irish Silver Assay Office Marks
        1544—1954. London 1955.
Jackson, C. J.: English Goldsmiths and their Marks. London
        1949.
Taylor, G.: Silver. Harmondsworth 1956.
Watts, W. W.: Old English Plate. 1924.

FINLAND

14th century — Finland was occupied by Sweden.

1743 — part of the country was occupied by Russia.

1809 — the whole country was occupied by Russia. Until this year, Swedish hallmarking was valid on the territory of Finland.

1810 — henceforth, new hallmarking was introduced (different from the Russian system: 1. state mark with the Finnish crown; 2. date letter (A = 1810; A2 = 1864; A3 = 1888, etc). 3. mark of purity in lots or zolotniks (13 L = 78 zolotniks = 812.5/1000); 4. maker's mark.

1920 — after liberalization, introduced in this year, the following purity became standard: 813 H = 830/1000; 916 H = 935/1000.

Bibliography:

Borg, Tyra: Guld och Silversmeder i Finland. Helsinki 1935.

FRANCE

1275 — a decree of Philip the Bold required the marking of silver objects with the town and maker's marks.

1577 — for fiscal reasons Henry III tried to introduce a new control hallmark (droit de remède).

1579 — Henry III; a new attempt to introduce another mark. Revenues from this mark were to be given to an assignee. The king's plan failed because of opposition by Parisian goldsmiths.

1672 — a new tax (droit de marque sur l'or et l'argent) was introduced. The collection of the tax was assigned and its payment was indicated on the object with a special mark.

1681 — another hallmark was added to the original single mark of the assignee. In practice hallmarking was carried out as follows (Rosenberg):

1. Before the maker completed the item, i. e. mainly before putting the parts together, he stamped each part of the object with his own mark, the so-called "poinçon à contre saign", later known as the "poinçon de maître".

2. The marked parts of the item were submitted in the "bureau de la régie" to the officials of an assignee who marked the product with a stamp known as "poinçon de charge". This mark indicated that the item was subject to taxation.
3. But the maker was not yet allowed to complete the item; he had now to submit it to the guild — "bureau de la maison commune" — where guild assayers (gardes des communautés) examined the fineness of the individual parts and stamped them with the town hallmark (usually also with the letter indicating the year), the so-called "poinçon de la maison commune".
4. The goldsmith could then complete the piece. Upon completion, however, and before selling it, he had to go to the "bureau de la régie" again where, after paying the assignee's fee, the item was stamped with the so-called "poinçon de décharge". Only then could the product be placed on sale. The object was therefore stamped with four marks. Since the hallmarks of the guild assayers and assignees changed according to the size of the object, according to the purity of the metal, according to the person of the assignee, and according to the revenue district (généralités), their number runs into thousands and to this day not all of them have been reliably ascertained.

1791 — the system of assignees was abolished and thus the "charge" and "décharge" marks disappeared.

1797 — a new system of hallmarking was introduced. The test of purity was taken over by the state. Henceforth purity was indicated by the "poinçon de titre", and payment of the revenue tax by the "poinçon de garantie".

Explanation of certain special terms:

Poinçon de reconnaissance — the hallmark of the assignees, introduced in 1750 to indicate newly added parts to an older object. Otherwise the name for various types of markings.

Poinçon de recense — new assignees could either retain the hallmarks of their predecessors, or have new ones made for them. In the event of a new hallmark being introduced, a general review was carried out in which objects that had been taxed by the predecessor of the new assignee were stamped with a special hallmark, free of charge. The first gratuituous review came about in 1722 when spurious assignee hallmarks were discovered.

Poinçon de vieux — a hallmark for older items which appeared for resale, but had been hallmarked earlier by an assignee.

Bibliography:

Boivin, J.: Les Anciens Orfèvres Français et leurs Poinçons. Paris 1923.

Carré, L.: Les Poinçons de l'Orfévrerie Française. Paris 1928.

Cripps, W. J.: Old French Plate. London 1893.

Nocq, H.: Les Poinçons de Paris. Paris 1926.

Tardy: Les Poinçons de garantie internationaux pour l'argent. Paris 1974.

GERMANY

1289 — first mention of hallmarking objects in Erfurt.

1548 — an imperial law was issued on the basis of which all objects weighing more than 4 lots and produced from 14 lot silver had to be submitted for assay and provided with the mark of the maker and that of the town, or possibly the nobleman on whose territory the goldsmith had settled.

1667 — the stipulations found in the imperial law of 1548 were repeated.

1888 — on 1 January uniform hallmarks were introduced throughout the territory of Germany. Since that time, objects were hallmarked as follows:
1. maker's mark; 2. purity in figures (in thousandths); 3. crescent mark with a crown (stamped by the maker himself if the silver is of higher purity than 800/1000).

Bibliography:

Rosenberg, M.: Der Goldschmiede Merkzeichen. Frankfurt a. M. 1922.

Scheffler, W.: Goldschmiede Niedersachsens. Berlin 1965.
Stierling, H.: Goldschmiedezeichen von Altona bis Tondern.
   Neumünster 1955.

GREECE

Regulations for controlling the purity of objects made of
   precious metals did not exist until the 1930s: that
   is, until the end of the period covered by this book.
   According to a police regulation, goldsmiths
   were obliged to register their names and their
   marks with the local authorities of the town and
   inform the police of the purchase and sale of
   precious metals.

HUNGARY

1500 — until 1500 hallmarking was not customary in
   Hungary. Some objects from the 14th and 15th
   centuries bear hallmarks but neither their significance, nor the system of hallmarking, has
   as yet been clarified.
1504 — the oldest regulation on hallmarking in Hungary
   was issued by Vladislav, the King of Bohemia,
   Poland and Hungary. The mark is called
   "signum communae czechae". It was stamped
   next to the maker's mark. From the name of the
   mark it is evident that the purity control was
   carried out by the guild. This system was valid on
   the territory of Hungary (and Slovakia, which
   until 1918 was part of Hungary) until 1866.
1866 — 1 August, a new system of hallmarking was
   introduced, valid for the whole territory of the
   former Austro-Hungarian Empire (see Austria).
   These marks were in force on Hungarian territory
   until 1937.

Bibliography:
Köszeghy, E.: Merkzeichen der Goldschmiede Ungarns vom
   Mittelalter bis 1867. Budapest 1936.

IRELAND

1495 — adoption of English regulations of 1423.

1498 — a goldsmiths' guild existed in Dublin.

1557 — the manufacture of precious metals was liberalized in Dublin.

1605 — the test of purity was renewed in Dublin because liberalization had been abused.

1637 — Charles I approved the statutes of the goldsmiths' guild in Dublin, valid for the whole of Ireland. It was decreed that the purity of silver must not be lower than the English standard.

1638 — introduction of date letters.

1729 — introduction of a "duty" tax from 25 March, 1730. Payment of the tax was confirmed on the object by stamping with the "Hibernia" marks.

1807 — Ireland adopted the English hallmarking system, following the Act of Union with England in 1800.

1923 — new marks were introduced from 4 April, 1923, after the restoration of independence. Henceforth, objects were marked as follows: 1. maker's mark; 2. town mark; 3. mark of purity; 4. date letter.

ITALY

The disintegration of the ancient Roman empire into small, free territories or towns prevented the introduction of a uniform system of hallmarking on the territory of present-day Italy until modern times. In towns, the guilds usually stamped their hallmarks; territorial states introduced their own hallmarking systems.

1797 — the Republic of Venice on whose territory there had been a uniform system of hallmarking, organized by the state, came to an end. In addition to the city of Venice, this territory included Verona, Brescia, Bergamo and Friuli, part of Istria and nearly the whole of Dalmatia.

1810 — a decree by Napoleon introduced into the Kingdom of Italy a hallmarking system based on the French model, with guarantee offices in Milan, Venice, Ancona, Verona and Brescia.

1815—59 (1866) — the French system remained in force on the territory occupied by Austria (Kingdom of Lombardy-Venice). Hallmarking offices were set up in Milan and Venice.

1818—72 — a special system of hallmarking was valid in the principalities of Modena and Parma during this period.

1873 — according to the law of 2 May, 1872, uniform hallmarking for the whole of Italy became valid. Manufacture was liberalized, the control of purity was not obligatory. Purities of 950, 900 and 800/1000 were introduced.

1935 — introduction of new marks and purities of 925 and 800/1000 valid to this day.

Bibliography:

Bulgari, C. G.: Argentieri, gemmari e orfi d'Italia. Roma 1958—69.

Sidney, J. A. — Churchill: The Goldsmiths of Italy. London 1926.

JAPAN

In Japan the hallmarking of objects made of precious metals was introduced in 1928 by the ministerial decree No 12 of 29 June. It was revised on 18 May, 1954. The permitted purity is given in thousandths in the following values: 1000, 950, 925, 900 and 800/1000. Silver objects must be marked according to the following specimen:

1. maker's mark; 2. control mark; 3. hallmark showing fineness.

NETHERLANDS

Until the wars of liberation against the Spaniards, the regulations applying to Spanish provinces were in force on the territory of the present-day Netherlands.

1501 — Archduke Philip issued goldsmiths' regulations for Holland, Seeland and Friesland (see Belgium).

1661 — the "Placaat en Ordonnante" was issued introducing the function of sworn assayers. These added to the maker's mark the town mark (merk van Stads Wapen) and a hallmark with the crowned lion (Provincialen gekroonden Leeuw), which guaranteed a higher content of precious metal (875/1000). Thus, on big pieces four marks were stamped according to this specimen:

1. town mark (Amsterdam); 2. date letter (in this instance 1608); 3. crowned lion; 4. maker's mark. For smaller items the maker's mark and the hallmark with the lion were required.

1806—10 — Kingdom of the Netherlands: new hallmarks for purities of 934 and 833/1000 and new date letters were established.

1810—14 — The Netherlands were joined to France.

1811 — the French system of hallmarking was introduced on the Emperor's orders. The items were marked with 1. the maker's mark; 2. a mark of purity; 3. the mark "bureau de garantie" (see France).

1814 — a royal decree established new marks valid only on the territory of the present-day Netherlands. On the territory of present-day Belgium, which until 1830 was part of the Netherlands, other hallmarks were used. Marks from 1814 were valid until 1953.

Bibliography:

Voet, E. Jr. and P. W. Voet: Nederlandse Goud- en Zilvermerken 1445—1951. The Hague 1951.

Voet, E.: Nederlandse Goud- en Zilversmeden, 1445—1951. The Hague 1963.

NORWAY

1314 — King Haakon V of Norway issued a decree requiring silver to be stamped with a purity mark.

1380—1814 — the union of Norway and Denmark — Danish regulations were in force.

1568 — a goldsmiths' guild was founded in Bergen.

1640—1740 — guilds were abolished and goldsmiths were directly subordinated to the king.

1740—1840 — the guilds were allowed again but their powers were very much curtailed.

1740 — henceforth hallmarks appeared for the individual months, first in the form of a fraction.

1766—1820 — hallmarks for the individual months depicted the signs of the zodiac.

A specimen of hallmarking from this period:

1. town mark (Bergen); 2. maker's mark (P. A. Aasmundsen); 3. mark of the year (1812); 4. assayer's mark (M. Pettersen); 5. mark of the month.

1859 — the guilds were once more abolished.

1891 — the law of 6 June introduced a modern system of hallmarking. The hallmark must have the purity in thousandths, the letter "S" next to the mark of purity, and the name of the maker. The lowest permitted purity is 830/1000.

Specimen:

830 S

name of the maker

The hallmark of officially assayed purity is the Norwegian lion with a crown.
The assay is optional.

Bibliography:

Vestlandske Kunstindustrimuseums Aarborg for Aaret 1903. Bergen 1903.

Krohn, H. T.: Trondhejms Gullsmedkunst 1550—1850. Oslo 1963.

POLAND

1548 — town marks are said to have been introduced by Sigismund August. Evidently a uniform hallmarking system was not yet in force. The hallmarking systems and marks changed with the different regimes in the territory of Poland:

1772 — the First Partition of Poland. Prussia occupied Polish Pomerania and western Prussia (except for Gdansk and Torun) and part of Great Poland. Austria seized Galicia (without Cracow), and Russia the territory at the Upper Dvina and the Dnieper.

1793 — the Second Partition of Poland. Prussia took Gdansk, Torun, most of Great Poland, Kujawy and Mazowsze, Russia the rest of White Russia, Podolye, Volhynia and the Ukraine.

1795 — the Third Partition of Poland. Russia seized the territory as far as the Bug and Niemen rivers, Prussia the rest of Great Poland with Warsaw, and Austria the whole of Little Poland with Cracow. Poland as an independent state ceased to exist.

1815—63 — following Napoleon's defeat, a new Polish Kingdom was created, ruled by the Russian Tsar. Galicia continued to remain under

Austrian administration, just as Prussia retained most of the territory it had seized earlier. Cracow and environs were declared a free republic.

1846 — Cracow was occupied by Austria. Until 1918 it remained part of the Austro-Hungarian Empire.

1863 — following the Warsaw Rising, the special privileges of the Polish Kingdom were abolished and it was then administered as the Russian Vistula Territory.

1920 — after the re-establishment of Poland, new hallmarks were introduced on 9 August. Permitted purities were 940, 875, 800/1000. These marks were valid until 1947.

Bibliography:

Bujańska, J.: Stare Srebra. Cracow 1972.

Lepszy, L.: Przemysł złotniczy w Polsce. Cracow 1933.

Myszkówna, H.: Srebra Warszawskie XVIII i XIX wieku w zbiorach Muzeum Historycznego. Warsaw 1973.

PORTUGAL

Before the introduction of a state hallmarking system in 1881, the individual towns had their own marks. The maker's mark was also required. Town marks guaranteed a purity of 958/1000.

1881 — introduction of a provisional state hallmarking system.

1886 — introduction of obligatory control of purity by a decree of 1 June. Permitted purity 916 and 833/1000.

1938 — 1 January introduction of new marks valid to this day. The system of hallmarking has remained the same.

Bibliography:

Dos Santos, R. and I. Quilho: Ourivesaria Portuguesa. Lisbon 1959—60.

Vidal, Manuel Goncalves: Marcas de Contraste e Ourives Portugueses XV° — 1950. Lisbon 1958.

RUMANIA

Until modern times, nothing is known about the hallmarking
of objects made of precious metals in Rumania.
In Transylvania and Banat, Hungarian regulations
were applied until 1919 (see Hungary, also
Austria).

1906 — the law of 28 February introduced a modern
hallmarking system.
Pieces had to be stamped with a purity mark
(950, 800 and 750/1000) and a maker's mark.

1919 and 1937 — new marks were introduced, the purity
standards being the same as in the 1906 law.

Bibliography:

Nicolescu, C.: Argintăria laică şi religiosă in Tările Române
sec. 14.—19. Bucharest 1968.

Tafrali, O.: Le trésor byzantin et roumain du monastère de
Poutna. Paris 1925.

RUSSIA

1613 — the first mention of the hallmarking of silver.

1649 — a ban on hallmarking of low purity silver.

1700 — Peter the Great issued a decree on hallmarking
not only for Moscow but also for the provinces.
After this year the "imenniki" — the maker's
marks — appear.

1733 — a decree was issued stipulating the proportion of
silver and copper in the alloy: 72 zolotniks of
silver and 24 zolotniks of copper.

1729 — first records of the assay office in Moscow.

1735 — an assay office was set up in St Petersburg.

18th—19th centuries — in Moscow the following pro-
cedure was followed in marking silver items:
the maker stamped his "imennik" on the finished
product and then submitted it to the guild where
it was marked to indicate that it was of good
quality. Then the maker had the item tested in the
assay office, where the assayer stamped it with
the mark of Moscow and his own mark. In the
other towns of the country the objects were
marked as follows: 1. town mark, sometimes

giving the date; 2. maker's mark with the monogram of his name and sometimes also with the date, always however in a rectangular shield; 3. mark of purity in figures (in zolotniks), always in a rectangular shield.

1891 — uniform marks were introduced for the whole country. The hallmark included the monogram of the assay district administrator, in addition to a depiction of a woman's head.

1927 — a new law on hallmarking came into effect establishing new marks of purity calculated in thousandths.

Bibliography:

Goldberg, T., Mishukov, F., Platonova, N. and Postnikova-Loseva, N. N.: Russkoe zolotoe i serebryanoe delo XV—XX vekov. Moscow 1967.

Rothemund, B.: Verzeichnis der russischen Gold- und Silbermarken. Munich 1971.

SCOTLAND

1457 — James III stipulated the purity of plate silver as 916/1000.
1483 — James III decreed the use of makers' marks.
1489 — the purity standard used in Bruges was adopted.
1525 — the first goldsmiths' guild in Edinburgh.
1555 — renewal of the original Scots purity standard 11 oz (= 916.6/1000).
1681 — introduction of date letters. Letters A to Z were used, excluding J.
1707 — Union of Scotland and England.

Bibliography:

See England.

SPAIN

16th century — a royal decree was issued according to which silver of a purity of 11 dineros 4 granos (= 930/1000) was permitted in producing silver objects. Every goldsmith had to have his own mark. The "marcador" stamped the town mark.

1785 — henceforth the date can be found along with certain town marks.

1881 — commencing with this year the production of silver pieces was liberalized and was usually of lower purity. At the request of the seller or buyer, the purity could be tested by an official assayer (Fiel contraste). Two purities were distinguished: 1. primera ley — no less than 11 dineros = 916/1000; 2. segunda ley = no less than 9 dineros = 750/1000.

1934 — new marks were introduced and purity was determined in thousandths. Items are stamped with two marks: 1. producer's mark; 2. mark of purity.

Bibliography:

Riane, J. F.: The Industrial Arts in Spain. London 1879.

Sanchez, J.: Orfebrería Murciana. 1950.

Sentach, N.: Bosquejo Histórico sobre la orfebrería española. 1908.

SWEDEN

1485 — a letter to the imperial council mentioned stamping items with the maker's mark.

1529 — in the goldsmiths' order of Gustav Vasa the maker's mark was mentioned.

16th century — during this century the maker's mark appeared alongside the town mark.

1689 — the imperial assayer A. Grill, in Stockholm, introduced date letters.

1752 — the state took over the control of the purity of objects made of precious metals.

1758 — the chamber assembly introduced the use of date letters throughout the country (including Finland).

Specimen of hallmarking from this time:

1. town mark (Alingsås); 2. maker's mark (Per Svanander); 3. date letter (for 1782); 4. state control mark.

1860 — instead of marks with the town emblem, special letters were introduced for the different places with assay offices, corresponding to the first letter of the name of the town.

Bibliography:

Upmark, G.: Guld- och Silversmeder i Sverige 1520—1850. Stockholm 1925.

Schwedische Silberschmiederei 1520—1850. Gold-und Silberstempel. Stockholm 1963.

SWITZERLAND

1544 — the administration of Zürich attempted to impose Zürich regulations stipulating the purity of precious metals on the other towns and cantons.

1547 — the proposal of Zürich was adopted in Lucerne and perhaps in Uri, Basel and Solothurn, too.

1848 — the federal government issued a decree on a uniform standard of purity throughout the territory of Switzerland. The individual cantons, however, continued to use their own marks.

1880 — a federal law on the control and guarantee of the purity of silver. Permitted purity 935, 925, 900, 875, and 800/1000.

1882 — uniform marks came into force throughout Switzerland, according to the law of 1880.

1893 — altered marks became valid and were used until 1934. The letter in the shield indicates the seat of the control office.

Bibliography:

Rittmeyer, D. F.: Diverses Etudes sur les Orfèvres Suisses d'Appendzell, Rapperswiller, S. Gallen, Schaffhausen, Toggenburg, etc.

Roosen, Runge M.: Die Goldschmiede der Stadt Bern. Bern 1951.

TUNISIA

1856—1905 — during this period items were stamped with the following marks:

1. mark of purity "Sekka" (c. 900/1000);
2. mark of guarantee "Sahha"; 3. "Khales" mark giving the date.
1878—1905 — introduction of the assayer's mark (a star), stamped on the item when put on sale.
1905 — new marks were introduced on 25 July; permitted purity of 900 and 800/1000. These marks were valid until 1942.

TURKEY

In 1844 a purity of 900/1000 was introduced; previously a purity of 800/1000 was used. An assay was not obligatory, and in any case it was not always precise. From 1923 onwards new marks were introduced, the permitted standards of purity being 900 and 800/1000. The marks changed in 1928, 1938, 1942 while maintaining the same purity standards as of 1923.

U.S.A.

Government bodies, whether colonial, federal or of the individual states, never had any control over the craftsmen and never stipulated purity standards for the use of precious metals. Not even date letters for the item were required. Nonetheless, the cities of New York and Boston had their Societies or Guilds (similar to the European guilds) in which the silversmiths themselves set the standards for their own craft. Most likely other cities of the United States, too, had similar organizations of silversmiths. In Baltimore, in fact, an assay office was set up for precious metals, supervised by elected silversmiths. The marks on American historical silver are mainly those of the makers, consisting either of a monogram or the silversmith's full name. Sometimes this mark is complemented with the name of the place where the maker worked, or a numeral indicating the purity of the precious metal employed. Since no date letter was required, an item can be dated more precisely only by analyzing the decoration on it or by a stylistic appraisal of the entire piece.

Silver objects produced in modern times must have the maker's mark and the number of purity, indicating precisely the purity of the metal with a tolerance of 004/1000. The mark "STERLING" or "STERLING SILVER" indicates a purity of 925/1000.

When identifying American silver it is essential to ascertain precisely and carefully the maker's mark which, in this instance, is the sole reliable indicator since, in many cases, English or Irish products were passed off as American work. Before selling the item the falsifier, of course, removed all the official marks, leaving only that of the maker.

Bibliography:

Avery, L. C.: American Silver of the XVII. and XVIII. Centuries. New York 1920.

Ensko, S. G. C.: American Silversmiths and their Marks. New York 1937.

Graham, J., Jr.: Early American Silvermarks. New York 1936.

Thorn, C. J.: Handbook of American Silver and Pewter Marks. New York 1949.

YUGOSLAVIA

1834 — obligatory hallmarking was introduced in the former Kingdom of Serbia for items manufactured of precious metals.

1882 — the law of 17 July introduced a new system of hallmarking on the territory of the former Kingdom of Serbia with the establishment of provincial control offices. Permitted purities were 800 and 750/1000.

1919 — with the emergence of present-day Yugoslavia, new hallmarks were introduced, valid for the entire country. Permitted purities are 900, 800 and 750/1000.

1933 — new hallmarks were introduced along with new purity standards of 950, 900 and 800/1000.

TABLE
OF FORMER PURITY
INDICATIONS:

1 lot = 062.5/1000		1 denier = 083.3/1000
12 lots = 750/1000		8 deniers = 666.6/1000
13 lots = 812.5/1000		9 deniers = 750/1000
14 lots = 875/1000		10 deniers = 833.3/1000
15 lots = 937,5/1000		11 deniers = 916.6/1000
16 lots = 1000/1000		12 deniers = 1000/1000

1 zolotnik = 010.4/1000	24 granos = 1 dinero
84 zolotniks = 875/1000	9 dineros = 750/1000
94 zolotniks = 980/1000	11 dineros = 916.6/1000
96 zolotniks = 1000/1000	12 dineros = 1000/1000

20 dwt (pennyweight) = 1 oz (ounce) Troy
11 oz 2 dwt = 925/1000 = Sterling Standard
11 oz 10 dwt = 958.3/1000 = Britannia Standard
12 oz 0. dwt = 1000/1000

Advice to readers:

1. Look for the mark according to what it depicts. Carefully identify, and if uncertain as to the depiction, compare it with similar subjects. Bear in mind that hallmarks usually have many variations which may differ from one another in minor details, and that in the course of time they may have become difficult to decipher. There are also many hallmarks showing several items or motifs. When deciphering the marks, therefore, take careful note of everything they contain.

2. When you have identified the mark with the help of this book, look at the hallmarking system of that particular country at the beginning of the book. An object usually bears more than one mark, the exact number corresponding to local regulations. You can then be certain that you have identified it correctly.

3. Next to each town or area the name of the country to which it now belongs is given. The present situation has been strictly adhered to because the borders of countries were often extremely fluid in historical times and some towns or territories changed hands many times. The names of the towns are given as they are used today, and the historical names appear in brackets.

4. International research on silver hallmarks has by no means ended, and therefore modern specialized literature is not uniform either as to the details of the marks or their dating. The author had no choice but to always keep to a single source which he regarded as the most important.

PLATES

ABBREVIATIONS
OF STATES:

A	=	Austria
B	=	Belgium
BG	=	Bulgaria
CH	=	Switzerland
CS	=	Czechoslovakia
D	=	Federal Republic of Germany
DDR	=	German Democratic Republic
DK	=	Denmark
E	=	Spain
ET	=	Egypt
F	=	France
GB	=	Great Britain
H	=	Hungary
I	=	Italy
IRL	=	Ireland
N	=	Norway
NL	=	Netherlands
P	=	Portugal
PL	=	Poland
R	=	Rumania
S	=	Sweden
SF	=	Finland
SU	=	Soviet Union
TN	=	Tunisia
USA	=	United States of America
YU	=	Yugoslavia

1 2	PARMA (I), 1818—1872, *larger and smaller items*
3	PARIS (F), 1684—1697, *contremarque — small items*
4	AURICH (D), 19th century
5	BELGIUM, 1869—1942, *state mark of purity 900/1000, smaller items*
6	BELGIUM, 1869—1942, *state mark of purity 800/1000, smaller items*
7	BELGIUM, 1869—1942, *state mark of purity 900/1000, larger items*
8	BELGIUM, 1869—1942, *state mark of purity 800/1000, larger items*
9	PARIS (F), "maison commune" for 1764
10	PARIS (F), 1744—1750, *charge*
11	AUDENARDE (Oudenaarde) (B), from the beginning of 18th century

12		PARIS (F), "maison commune" for 1644
13		PARIS (F), 1750—1756, *charge*
14		PARIS (F), 1704—1712, *charge*
15		PARIS (F), 1727—1732, *charge*
16		PARIS (F), 1727—1732, *charge*
17		PARIS-GÉNÉRALITÉ (F), (revenue district), 1756—1762, *charge*
18		PARIS (F), 1768—1774, *charge — large items*
19		PARIS-GÉNÉRALITÉ (F), (revenue district), 1756—1762, *charge*
20		PARIS-GÉNÉRALITÉ (F), (revenue district), 1780—1791, *charge*
21		PARIS (F), 1713—1717, *charge*

22	PARIS (F), 1756—1762, *charge — large items*
23	PARIS (F), 1713—1717, *charge*
24	PARIS (F), 1738—1744, *charge*
25	PARIS (F), 1762—1768, *charge — large items*
26	PARIS-GÉNÉRALITÉ (F), (revenue district), 1780—1791, *charge —* large items
27	PARIS (F), 1781—1789, *charge — large items*
28	PARIS (F), 1775—1781, *charge — large items*
29	PARIS (F), 1783, *charge — large items*
30	PARIS (F), 1732—1738, *charge*
31	PARIS (F), 1722—1727, *charge — large items*

32		PARIS (F), 1717—1722, *charge*
33		METZ (F), 1780—1791, *charge — large items*
34		METZ (F), 1774—1780, *charge — large items*
35		PARIS (F), 1704—1712, *décharge*
36		PARIS (F), 1713—1717, *décharge*
37		SALINS (F), 1784
38		PARIS (F), 1684—1687, *small items*
39		PARIS (F), 1687—1691, *charge — large items*
40		PARIS (F), 1691—1698, *décharge*
41		PARIS (F), 1691—1698, *décharge — small items*

42		PARIS (F), 1691—1698, *charge*
43		PARIS (F), 1697—1703, *charge — large items*
44		ROUEN (F), 1780—1789, *charge — minor items*
45		PARIS (F), 1687—1691, *control mark*
46		VÄSTERÅS (S), 17th—19th centuries
47		PARIS (F), 1684—1687, *contremarque — larger items*
48		PARIS (F), 1684—1687, *older items*
49		PARIS (F), 1677—1680, *charge — large items*
50		PARIS (F), 1680—1684, *charge — large items*
51		MANTES (F), 1748

52		PARIS (F), 1684—1687, *charge — large items*
53		PARIS (F), 1684—1687, *charge — small items*
54		PARIS (F), 1677—1680, *charge — large items*
55		MEAUX (F), 1750
56 57 58		HUNGARY, 1937—1965, *export mark; purity 935/1000 purity 900/1000 purity 800/1000*
59		ALINGSÅS (S), mid-18th century
60		U.S.A., Abel Buel, 1742—1825, *New Haven, Conn.*
61		U.S.A., Adrien Bancker, 1703—1772, *New York, N. Y.*
62		ABERDEEN (GB), 17th—18th centuries, *many variations*
63		ABERDEEN (GB), 18th century, *many variations*

64		U.S.A., Arnold Collins, 1690 *Newport, R.I.*
65		U.S.A., Alexander Camman, 1813, *Albany, N.Y.*
66		U.S.A., Albert Cole, 1844, *New York, N.Y.*
67		CAEN (F), 1780— 1791, *charge — minor items*
68		MONS (Bergen) (B), 17th—18th centuries
69		SPAIN, from 1934, *export mark*
70		AGUILAR (E), 17th century
71		U.S.A., Abraham Portram, 1727, *New York, N.Y.*
72		L'AQUILA (I), 15th century
73		L'AQUILA (I), 16th century
74		U.S.A., Richard Andras, 1797, *New York, N.Y.*

75		AARHUS (DK), 17th century
76		BAYONNE (F), 1780—1789, *charge — minor items*
77		AMIENS (F), 1780—1790, *charge — minor items*
78		U.S.A., Andrew Tyler, 1692—1741, *Boston, Mass.*
79 80		FORMER AUSTRO-HUNGARIAN EMPIRE, 1872—1902, *import mark*

Key to the Marks:
A — Vienna (A)
B — Linz (A)
C — Prague (CS)
D — Brno (CS)
E — Cracow (PL)
F — Lvov (SU)
G — Graz (A)
H — Bregenz (A)
K — Klagenfurt (A)
L — Ljubljana (YU)
M — Trieste
P — Pest (H)
R — Košice (CS)
T — Timişoara (R)
U — Alba Iulia (R)
V — Zagreb (YU)

LETTER B

81 82	**B** B	PIACENZA (I), 1818—1872, *larger and smaller items*

83		BAMBERG (D), 17th—18th centuries
84		FORMER AUSTRO-HUNGARIAN EMPIRE, 1806—1809, *restamped mark for small items*

Key to the Marks:
A — Vienna (A)
B — Prague (CS)
C — Salzburg (A)
D — Lvov (SU)
E — Cracow (PL)
F — Brno (CS)
G — Linz (A)
H — Graz (A)
I — Klagenfurt (A)
K — Ljubljana (YU)
L — Trieste

85		BRZEG (Brieg) (PL), 18th century
86		BRUGES (B), c. 1660
87		BORÅS (S), 1745
88		U.S.A., Thanvet Besley, 1727, *New York, N.Y.*
89		BESANÇON (F), 18th century
90		ROUEN (F), 1698, *charge*

91		PAU (F), 18th century
92		TROYES (F), 1774—1780
93		PARIS (F), "maison commune" for 1765
94		PARIS (F), "maison commune" for 1695
95		SENS (F), 1749
96		PARIS (F), "maison commune" for 1670
97		PARIS (F), "maison commune" for 1742
98		ROUEN (F), 1698, *charge*
99		BORDEAUX (F), 1780—1789, *charge — minor items*
100		BOURGES (F) 1780—1789, *charge — minor items*

101		ROUEN (F), 1780—1789, *charge — large items*
102		ROUEN (F), 1774—1780, *charge — large items*
103		PARIS (F), "maison commune" for 1507
104		ROUEN (F), 1768—1774, *charge*
105		BESANÇON (F), late 17th century
106		MANTES (F), 1756
107		ETAMPES (F), 1762
108		VERSAILLES (F), 1746
109		BRAGA (P), 1886—1888
110		BARCELONA (E), 16th—17th centuries

111		BARCELONA (E), 16th—17th centuries
112		BARCELONA (E), 15th century
113		U.S.A., Garrett Onclebagh, 1698, *New York, N.Y.*
114		U.S.A., Benjamin Hiller, 1687, *Boston, Mass.*
115		U.S.A., Benjamin Hurd, 1739—1781, *Boston, Mass.*
116		U.S.A., John Brevoort, 1715—1775, *New York, N.Y.*
117		U.S.A., Bartholomew Le Roux, 1688—1713, *New York, N.Y.*
118		U.S.A., Brower and Rusher, 1834, *New York, N.Y.*
119		BREVIK (N), 18th century
120		BURGOS (E), 16th century
121		U.S.A., Barnebus Webb, 1762, *Boston, Mass.*
122		U.S.A., B. Ward, 1729—1777, *Guilford, Conn.*

123	B&W	U.S.A., Beach and Ward, 1789—1795, *Hartford, Conn.*

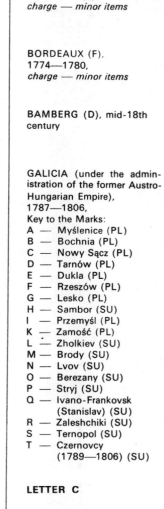

124		BOURGES (F), 1774—1780, *charge — minor items*
125		BORDEAUX (F), 1774—1780, *charge — minor items*
126		BAMBERG (D), mid-18th century
127		GALICIA (under the administration of the former Austro-Hungarian Empire), 1787—1806,

Key to the Marks:
A — Myślenice (PL)
B — Bochnia (PL)
C — Nowy Sącz (PL)
D — Tarnów (PL)
E — Dukla (PL)
F — Rzeszów (PL)
G — Lesko (PL)
H — Sambor (SU)
I — Przemyśl (PL)
K — Zamość (PL)
L — Zholkiev (SU)
M — Brody (SU)
N — Lvov (SU)
O — Berezany (SU)
P — Stryj (SU)
Q — Ivano-Frankovsk (Stanislav) (SU)
R — Zaleshchiki (SU)
S — Ternopol (SU)
T — Czernovcy (1789—1806) (SU)

LETTER C

128		KULMBACH (D), 16th—17th centuries

129		KARLSTAD (S), 18th—19th centuries
130		CAEN (F), 1744—1750, *charge — large items*
131		PARIS (F), "maison commune" for 1743
132		BESANÇON (F), 1764
133		CAEN (F), 1744—1780, *charge — large items*
134		CAEN (F), 1730—1791, *charge — large items*
135		KRISTIANSTAD (S), 18th—19th centuries
136		OSLO (former Kristiania) (N), 1624—c. 1820, *the numeral signifies the year, here 1747; after 1712 the full date is sometimes given*
137		CALATAYUD (E), 16th century
138		CASTELLÓN DE LA PLANA (E), 16th—17th centuries
139		U.S.A., Charles Le Roux, 1689—1745, *New York, N.Y.*

140		U.S.A., Charles Candell, 1795, *New York, N.Y.*
141		U.S.A., Charters, Cann and Dunn, 1850, *New York, N.Y.*
142		CERVANTES or CERVERA (E) 15th—17th centuries
143		CAEN (F), 1774—1780, *charge — minor items*
144		U.S.A., Cornelius Kiersteade, 1753, *New York, N.Y.*
145		LARVIK (N), 18th century
146		U.S.A., Charles L. Boehme, 1774—1868, *Baltimore, Md.*
147		CÓRDOBA (E), 15th—16th centuries
148		U.S.A., Cleveland and Post, 1815, *Norwich, Conn.*
149		U.S.A., Forbes, V. G. Collins, 1816, *New York, N.Y.*
150		GRENOBLE (F), 1775—1780, *charge — minor items*

151		DESSAU (D), 18th—19th centuries
152		LYON (F), 1688—1703, *charge*
153		PARIS (F), "maison commune" for 1744
154		BESANÇON (F), 1765
155		DIJON (F), 1780—1791, *charge — minor items*
156		LYON (F), 1780—1791, *charge — large items*
157		LYON (F), 1775—1780, *charge — large items*
158		LYON (F), 1762—1768, *charge*
159		LYON (F), 1768—1775, *charge — large items*

160		LYON (F), 1756—1762, *charge*
161		LYON (F), 17th century, *charge*
162		U.S.A., Daniel Boyer, 1726—1779, *Boston, Mass.*
163		U.S.A., Bayley and Douglas, 1789, *New York, N.Y.*
164		U.S.A., Dupuy and Sons, 1784, *Philadeplhia, Pa.*
165		U.S.A., David Jesse, 1670—1705, *Boston, Mass.*
166		U.S.A., D. Maverick, 1828, *New York, N. Y.*
167		U.S.A., Downing and Phelps, 1810, *New York, N.Y.*
168		VERSAILLES (F), 1770
169		**LETTER E** ERFURT (DDR), 16th—18th centuries, *the shield changes shape*

170		TOURS (F), 1768—1774, *charge*
171		PARIS (F), "maison commune" for 1745
172		PARIS (F), "maison commune" for 1721
173		TOURS (F), early 18th century, *charge*
174		TOURS (F), 1751—1756, *charge*
175		PARIS (F), "maison commune" for 1673
176		PARIS (F), "maison commune" for 1649
177		PARIS (F), 1704—1712, *contremarque — review*
178		BESANÇON (F), 1768

179		TOURS (F), 1774—1780, *charge — large items*
180		TOURS (F), 1780—1789, *charge — large items*
181		PARIS (F), 1749—1774, *import mark*
182		PARIS (F), "maison commune" for 1745
183		BESANÇON (F), 1794—1797
184		TOURS (F), 1762—1768, *charge*
185		PARIS (F), 1749—1774, *import mark*
186		EMDEN (D), 1820
187		PARIS (F), "maison commune" for 1511

188	BELGIUM, 1831—1869, *import mark*
189	EKSJÖ (S), early 18th century
190	U.S.A., Ephraim Brasher, 1766, *New York, N.Y.*
191	U.S.A., Esekiel Buer, 1764—1846, *Providence, R.I.*
192	U.S.A., Eliphaz Hart, 1789—1866, *Norwich, Conn.*
193	U.S.A., Eliakim Hitshcock, 1752, *Boston, Mass.*
194	U.S.A., Edgar M. Eoff, 1735—1758, *New York, N.Y.*
195	SWITZERLAND, "Poinçon de Notoriété", imitation of French 18th-century marks
196	U.S.A., Edward Pear, 1836, *Boston, Mass.*
197	U.S.A., Eoff and Phyfe, 1844, *New York, N.Y.*
198	ITALY, 1810—1872, *import mark*

199		ASTORGA (E), 16th century
200		FRANCE, 1798—1809, *import mark for small items*
201		ÉVORA (P), 18th—19th centuries
202		VERSAILLES (F), 1775—1781
203		MELUN (F), 2nd half of 18th century
204		U.S.A., Edward Winslow, 1669—1753, *Boston, Mass.*

LETTER F

205		FORSSA (SF), up to 1943
206		FREIBERG (DDR), 17th century
207		PARIS (F), "maison commune" for 1746
208		PARIS (F), "maison commune" for 1769

209		FLORENCE (I), 18th century
210		BESANÇON (F), 1767
211		PARIS (F), "maison commune" for 1722
212		ANGERS (F), 1780—1789, *charge*
213		CHARTRES (F), 1747
214		PARIS (F), "maison commune" for 1674
215		PARIS (F), "maison commune" for 1722
216	F.&G.	U.S.A., Fletcher and Bardiner, 1812, *Philadelphia, Pa.*
217	F.&M	U.S.A., Frost and Mumford, 1810, *Providence, R. I.*
218	FR	U.S.A., Francis Richardson, 1718, *Philadelphia, Pa.*

219		FREDRIKSSTAD (N), 2nd half of 17th century
220		PRUSSIA, revenue mark for items manufactured prior to 12 February, 1809
		LETTER G
221		GÄVLE (S), 18th—19th centuries
222		PARIS (F), "maison commune" for 1723
223		GHENT (B), 18th century
224		GOTHA (DDR), 17th century
225		GÖTEBORG (S), 19th century
226		POITIERS (F), 1680
227		PARIS (F), "maison commune" for 1675

228	GUIMARÃES (P), late 18th century
229	POITIERS (F), 1774—1780, *charge — large items*
230	POITIERS (F), 1755
231	POITIERS (F), 1780—1791, *charge — large items*
232	GÄVLE (S), late 17th century
233	GRENOBLE (F), 1780—1791, *charge — minor items*
234	U.S.A., George Bardick, 1790, *Philadelphia, Pa.*
235	GÖTEBORG (S), 17th—18th centuries
236	GERONA (E), 16th century
237	U.S.A., George Hanners, 1697, *Boston, Mass.*

238		U.S.A., Gabriel Lewyn, 1771, *Baltimore, Md.*
239		U.S.A., George Stephens, 1790, *New York, N.Y.*
240		U.S.A., George Tyler, 1740—1785, *Boston, Mass.*
241		GÖRLITZ (DDR), 18th century
242		PARIS-GÉNÉRALITÉ (F), (revenue district), 1781—1790, *charge — minor items*

LETTER H

243		HÄRNÖSAND (S), 18th—19th centuries
244		HÄRNÖSAND (S), 18th—19th centuries
245		PARIS (F), "maison commune" for 1771
246		PARIS (F), "maison commune" for 1724
247		LA ROCHELLE (F), 1780—1791, *charge — large items*

248		LA ROCHELLE (F), 1774—1780, *charge — large items*
249		HAPARANDA (S), 19th century
250		U.S.A., Henry Andrews, 1795, *Philadelphia, Pa*.
251		HEILBRONN (D), early 18th century
252		U.S.A., Henricus Boelen, 1684—1755, *New York, N.Y*.
253		U.S.A., Henry Hurst, 1665—1717, *Boston, Mass*.
254		U.S.A., Hall and Hewson, 1819, *Albany, N. Y*.
255		U.S.A., Henry Loring, 1773—1818, *Boston, Mass*.
256		U.S.A., Hays and Myers, 1770, *New York, N. Y*.
257		U.S.A., Henry Pitkin, 1834, *East Hartford, Conn*.
258		U.S.A., Henry R. Traux, 1815, Albany, N.Y.

259		KARKKILA (SF), up to 1943

LETTER I

260		IISALMI (SF), up to 1943
261		PARIS (F), 1677—1680, *charge — large items*
262		PARIS (F), "maison commune" for 1725
263		LIMOGES (F), 1774—1780, *charge — large items*
264		LIMOGES (F), 1780—1791, *charge — large items*
265		U.S.A., I. Adam, 1800 *Alexandria, Va.*
266		U.S.A., John Benjamin, 1731—1796, *Stratford, Conn.*
267		U.S.A., John Burt, 1691—1745, *Boston, Mass.*
268		U.S.A., Jacob Boelen, 1773, *New York, N.Y.*

269		U.S.A., John Carman, 1771, *Philadelphia, Pa.*
270		U.S.A., I. Clark, 1754, *Boston, Mass.*
271		U.S.A., John Coney, 1655—1722, *Boston, Mass.*
272		U.S.A., John Coney, 1655—1722, *Boston, Mass.*
273		U.S.A., John Coddington, 1690—1743, *Newport, R.I.*
274		U.S.A., John Dixwell, 1680—1725, *Boston, Mass.*
275		U.S.A., John David, 1736—1794, *Philadelphia, Pa.*
276		U.S.A., Jonathan Davenport, 1789—1801, *Baltimore, Md.*
277		U.S.A., John Edwards, 1700, *Boston, Mass.*
278		U.S.A., John Edwards, 1700, *Boston, Mass.*

279		U.S.A., Joseph Goldthwaite 1706—1780, *Boston, Mass.*
280		U.S.A., Jacob B. Lansing, 1736, *Albany, N.Y.*
281		U.S.A., John Hull, 1624—1683, *Boston, Mass.*
282		U.S.A., John Hastier, 1726, *New York, N.Y.*
283		U.S.A., John Inch, 1720—1763, *Annapolis, Md.*
284		IKAALINEN (SF), up to 1943
285		U.S.A., Joseph Keeler, 1786—1824, *Norwalk, Conn.*
286		ILMAJOKI (SF), up to 1943
287		U.S.A., John Lyng, 1734, *Philadelphia, Pa.*
288		U.S.A., John Denise, 1698, *Philadelphia, Pa.*
289		U.S.A., John Noyes, 1695, *Boston, Mass.*

290	**IP**	CZECHOSLOVAKIA, inventory mark of 1929, for *purity 950—650/1000*
291	**IP**	U.S.A., Isaac Perkins, 1707, *Charlestown, Mass.*
292	**IR**	U.S.A., Jonathan Reed, 1725—1740, *Boston, Mass.*
293	**IW**	U.S.A., Isaiah Wagster, 1776—1793, *Baltimore, Md.*

LETTER J

294	**J.A & I.A**	U.S.A., Joseph Anthony and Sons, 1810, *Philadelphia, Pa.*
295	**J.B**	U.S.A., John Boyce, 1801, *New York, N.Y.*
296	**JC**	U.S.A., Jonathan Crosby, 1743—1769, *Boston, Mass.*
297	**J:D**	U.S.A., John Denise, 1798, *New York, N. Y.*
298	**J**	DIJON (F), 1774—1780, *charge — minor items*
299	**J+M**	U.S.A., Joseph Moulton II, 1757, *Newburyport, Mass.*

300		U.S.A., Joseph Phillipe, 1796, *Baltimore, Md*.
301		U.S.A., Joseph P. Warner, 1811—1862, *Baltimore, Md*.
302		U.S.A., John Starr Blackman, 1777—1851, *Danbury, Conn*.
303		U.S.A., John Wendover, 1694, *New York, N.Y*.
304		U.S.A., Joseph W. Boyd, 1820, *New York, N.Y*.
305		U.S.A., J. W. Faulkner, 1835, *New York, N.Y*.

LETTER K

306		KARLSHAMN (S), lst half of 18th century
307		PARIS (F), "maison commune" for 1750
308		PARIS (F), "maison commune" for 1773
309		PARIS (F), "maison commune" for 1726

69

310	BORDEAUX (F), 1744—1750, *charge*
311	PARIS (F), 1677—1680, *charge — large items*
312	KØGE (DK), 18th century
313	LILLE (F), 1750, *date letter*
314	LILLE (F), 1776
315	BORDEAUX (F), 1756—1762, *charge*
316	BORDEAUX (F), 1738—1744, *charge*
317 318	BORDEAUX (F), 1768—1774, *charge*
319	PARIS (F), "maison commune" for 1726

320		BORDEAUX (F), 1698—1703, *charge*
321		BORDEAUX (F), 1774—1780, *charge*
322		BORDEAUX (F), 1780—1789, *charge — large items*
323		PARIS (F), "maison commune" for 1515
324		BORDEAUX (F), 1672—1680, *charge*
325		KUNGSBACKA (S), 18th—19th centuries
326		U.S.A., Krider and Biddle, 1830, *Philadelphia, Pa.*
327		U.S.A., Koenraet Ten Eyck, 1678—1735, *New York, N.Y.*
328		BORDEAUX (F), 1691—1698, *charge*
329		KIEV (SU), 1735—1774

330		KOTKA (SF), up to 1943
331		KASKINEN (SF), up to 1943
		LETTER L
332		LIEKSA (SF) and LOHJA (SF), up to 1943
333		LOVIISA (SF), up to 1943
334		LEIPZIG (DDR), 16th century up to the beginning of 18th century, many variations
335		OŁAWA (Ohlau) (PL), 17th—18th centuries
336		LISBON (P), 1881—1887, *minimum purity 750/1000*
337		LISBON (P), 1881—1887, *minimum purity 750/1000*
338		PARIS (F), "maison commune" for 1752
339		LISBON (P), 18th—19th centuries

340		LISBON (P), late 17th century
341		LISBON (P), 17th—18th centuries
342		BAYONNE (F), 1774—1780, *charge — large items*
343		LYON (F), 1780—1791, *charge — minor items*
344		TOURS (F), 1738—1744, *charge*
345		BAYONNE (F), mid-18th century
346		LAPUA (SF), up to 1943
347		U.S.A., Loring Bailey, 1780, Hingham, Mass.
348		LEÓN (E), 18th century
349		U.S.A., Lincoln and Green, 1810, *Boston, Mass.*

350		LAHTI (SF), up to 1943
351		BAYONNE (F), 1780—1789, *charge — large items*
352		VERSAILLES (F), 1780—1789 *charge — large items*
353		LOIMAA (SF), up to 1943
354		POTSDAM (DDR), 18th century, *mark of purity*
355		U.S.A., Lemuel Wells, 1791, *New York, N.Y.*
356		POITIERS (F), 1774—1780, *charge — minor items*
357		LA ROCHELLE (F), 1774—1780, *charge — small items*
358		VERSAILLES (F), 1780—1789, *charge — medium-sized items*
359		LIMOGES (F), 1780—1791, *charge — minor items*

360		PARIS (F), 1783, *charge — minor items*
361		PARIS (F), 1781—1789, *charge — medium-sized items*
362		LISBON (P), 1886—1888

LETTER M

363		MAARIANHAMINA (SF), up to 1943
364		MALMKÖPING (S), 19th century
365		TOULOUSE (F), 16th—17th centuries, *charge*
366		PARIS (F), "maison commune" for 1775
367		PARIS (F), maison commune" for 1752
368 369		MEXICO, 1770 *throughout the Spanish occupation*

370		TOULOUSE (F), 16th—17th centuries, *charge*
371 372		PALMA DE MALLORCA (E), 1881—1934, *for large items, for small items*
373		METZ (F), 1780—1791, *charge — small items*
374		TOULOUSE (F), 1768—1774, *charge*
375		TOULOUSE (F), 1768—1774, *charge*
376		TOULOUSE (F), 1774—1780, *charge — large items*
377		TOULOUSE (F), 1780—1789, *charge — large items*
378		TOULOUSE (F), 16th—17th centuries, *charge*
379		PARIS (F), "maison commune" for 1517

380		ANGERS (F), 1768—1774, *charge*
381		MANTES (F), 1743
382		TOULOUSE (F), 16th—17th centuries, *charge*
383		MALTA, 1623—1636
384		MEAUX (F), 1750, *middle letter changes according to year*
385		MEAUX (F), 1768, *middle letter changes according to year*
386		MEAUX (F), 1778, *middle letter changes according to year*
387 388		FORMER AUSTRO-HUNGARIAN EMPIRE, 1887, *hallmark for low sub-standard purity*
389		MARIEFRED (S), 18th century

390		U.S.A., Munson Jarvis, 1742—1824, *Stamford, Conn.*
391		U.S.A., Mathias Lamar, 1790, *Philadelphia, Pa.*
392		U.S.A., Marcus Merriman and Co., 1817, *New Haven, Conn.*
393		U.S.A., McFee and Reeder, 1796, *Philadelphia, Pa.*
394		METZ (F), 1774—1780, *charge — minor items*
395		AMIENS (F), 1774—1780, *charge — minor items*
396		LIMOGES (F), 1774—1780, *charge — minor items*
397		ORÉANS (F), 1780—1791, *charge — minor items*
398		LYON (F), 1775—1780, *charge — minor items*
399		BAYONNE (F), 1774—1780, *charge — minor items*

400		NUREMBERG (D), 1700—1750
401		PARIS (F), "maison commune" for 1682
402		PARIS (F), "maison commune" for 1753
403		NUREMBERG (D), 19th century
404		PARIS (F), "maison commune" for 1729
405		NUREMBERG (D), up to mid-16th century
406		NANTES (F), 1762—1769, *charge*
407		NANTES (F), 1769—1784, *charge*
408		NAPLES (I), 18th century, *changing date, here 1716*

409		NAPLES (I), 16th century,
410		NÆSTVED (DK), 17th—18th centuries
411		U.S.A., Nathaniel Morse, 1709, *Boston, Mass.*

LETTER O

412		OSTERODE (D), 17th—18th centuries
413		PARIS (F), "maison commune" for 1707
414		PARIS (F), "maison commune" for 1777
415		RIOM (F), 1774—1780, *charge — large items*
416		RIOM (F), 1780—1789, *charge — large items*
417		MONTEREAU (F), 1768—1774, *contremarque*

418		OSTERODE (D), 19th century
419		OCHSENFURT (D), 17th century
420		U.S.A., Otto Paul De Parisien, 1763, *New York, N.Y.*
421		U.S.A., O. Parisien and Son, 1789, *New York, N.Y.*
422		ORLÉANS (F), 1774—1780, *charge — minor items*
423		TOURS (F), 1774—1780, *charge — minor items*
424		RIOM (F), 1774—1780, *charge — minor items*

LETTER P

425		OPORTO (P), 18th century
426		OPORTO (P), mid-16th century
427		DIJON (F), 1756—1759, *charge*

428		NANTES (F), 1746, *charge*
429		OPORTO (P), 1881—1887, *minimum purity 750/1000*
430		OPORTO (P), 1886—1888
431		OPORTO (P), since 1891, *control mark for silver watches*
432		PARIS (F), "maison commune" for 1789
433		PARIS (F), "maison commune" for 1788
434		DIJON (F), 1775—1780, *charge — large items*
435		DIJON (F), 1780—1791, *charge — large items*
436		DIJON (F), 1691—1698, *charge*
437		PARIS (F), "maison commune" for 1788

438		PARIS (F), "maison commune" for 1784
439		DIJON (F), 1756—1759, *charge*
440		DIJON (F), 1759—1762, *charge*
441		PARIS (F), "maison commune" for 1785
442		DIJON (F), 1732—1744, *charge*
443		DIJON (F), 1759—1762, *charge*
444		PARIS (F), "maison commune" for 1786
445		DIJON (F), 1726—1732, *charge*
446		PARIS (F), "maison commune" for 1787
447		POITIERS (F), 1780—1791, *charge — minor items*

448		DIJON (F), 17th century, *charge*
449		DIJON (F), 1750—1756
450		PARIS (F), "maison commune" for 1787
451		PARIS (F), "maison commune" for 1784
452		PARIS (F), "maison commune" for 1785
453		PARIS (F), "maison commune" for 1786
454		PARIS (F), "maison commune" for 1789
455		PAU (F), early 18th century
456		U.S.A., Phineas Bradley, 1745—1797, *New Haven, Conn.*
457		U.S.A., Peter David, 1707—1755, *Philadelphia, Pa.*

458		BUDAPEST (H), 19th century, *for silver-plating on pipes*
459		U.S.A., Peter Feurt, 1731, *New York, N.Y.*
460		LENINGRAD (St Petersburg) (SU), 1873—1896, *changing date*
461		U.S.A., Parry and Musgrave, 1793, *Philadeplhia, Pa.*
462		U.S.A., Peter Oliver, 1709, *Bostòn, Mass.*
463		U.S.A., Peter Perreaux, 1797, *Philadelphia, Pa.*
464		U.S.A., Peter Quintard, 1731, *New York, N.Y.*
465		U.S.A., Paul Revere Sr., 1702—1754, *Boston, Mass.*
466		U.S.A., Paul Revere, 1735—1818, *Boston, Mass.*
467		U.S.A., Paul Revere, 1735—1818, *Boston, Mass.*
468		U.S.A., Philip Syng, 1703—1789, *Philadelphia, Pa.*

469	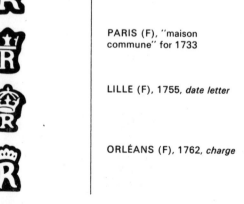	PARIS (F), 1775—1781, *charge — small items*

LETTER Q

470		PARIS (F), "maison commune" for 1709
471		BESANÇON (F), 1777
472		PARIS (F), "maison commune" for 1650
473		PARIS (F), "maison commune" for 1732

LETTER R

474		PARIS (F), "maison commune" for 1780
475	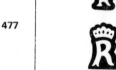	PARIS (F), "maison commune" for 1733
476		LILLE (F), 1755, *date letter*
477		ORLÉANS (F), 1762, *charge*

478		ROSKILDE (DK), 18th century
479		BESANÇON (F), 1778
480		ORLÉANS (F), 1780—1791, *charge — large items*
481		ORLÉANS (F), 1774—1780, *charge — large items*
482		ORLÉANS (F), 1732, *charge*
483		ORLÉANS (F), 1751—1762, *charge*
484		RENNES (F), 1780—1789, *charge — minor items*
485		RIOM (F), 1780—1789, *charge — minor items*
486		ORLÉANS (F), 1768—1774, *charge*
487		BELGIUM, 1831, *"review" — introduced during transition from the Dutch to the Belgian system of hallmarking*

488		ROSTOCK (DDR), late 16th century and 17th century
489		BELGIUM, 1831, *"review" — introduced during transition from the Dutch to the Belgian system of hallmarking*
490		U.S.A., Robert Brookhouse, 1750, *Salem, Mass.*
491		U.S.A., Joseph Conyers, 1708, *Boston, Mass.*
492		U.S.A., Robert Douglas, 1776, *New London, Conn.*
493		U.S.A., Rufus Greene, 1707—1777, *Boston, Mass.*
494		U.S.A., Rene Grignon, 1715, *Norwich, Conn.*
495		U.S.A., Riggs and Griffith, 1816, *Baltimore, Md.*
496		ROVANIEMI (SF), up to 1943
497		U.S.A., Robert Sanderson, 1693, *Boston, Mass.*
498		U.S.A., Richard Vincent, 1799, *Baltimore, Md.*

499		U.S.A., Robert Wilson, 1816, *New York, N.Y.*
500		LA ROCHELLE (F), 1780—1791, *charge — minor items*
501		RENNES (F), 1774—1780, *charge — minor items*
502		ROUEN (F), 1774—1780, *charge — minor items*

LETTER S

503		SALZBURG (A), 16th—17th centuries
504		SALZBURG (A), 18th century
505		SKIEN (N), 2nd half of 18th century
506		SKÖVDE (S), 18th century
507		PARIS (F), "maison commune" for 1758
508		PARIS (F), "maison commune" for 1781

509	STOCKHOLM (S), 1500—1600
510	SENLIS (F), 1723
511	PARIS (F), "maison commune" for 1734
512	LILLE (F), 1755, *date letter*
513	SCHWEINFURT (D), 18th century
514	SURSEE (CH), 17th—18th centuries
515	SURSEE (CH), 18th century
516	SURSEE (CH), early 17th century
517	U.S.A., Samuel Avery, 1760—1836, *Preston, Conn.*
518	SAKSKØBING (DK), c. 1696

519		TURKEY, 1928—1938, purity 900/1000
520		TURKEY, 1928—1938, purity 800/1000
521		U.S.A., Samuel Burt, 1724—1754, *Boston, Mass*.
522		U.S.A., Samuel Burrill, 1733, *Boston, Mass*.
523		U.S.A., Chaudrons, Simon and Co., 1807, *Philadelphia, Pa*.
524		U.S.A., Storrs and Cooley, 1832, *New York, N.Y*.
525		U.S.A., Shem Drowne, 1749, *Boston, Mass*.
526		U.S.A., Stephen Emory, 1725—1801, *Boston, Mass*.
527		U.S.A., Samuel Gilbert, 1798, *Hebron, Conn*.
528		U.S.A., Samuel Haugh, 1675—1717, *Boston, Mass*.
529		U.S.A., Jacobus van de Spiegel, 1668—1708, *New York, N. Y*.

530		U.S.A., Vanderspiegel, 1701, *New York, N.Y.*
531		U.S.A., Samuel Leach, 1741, *Philadelphia, Pa.*
532		U.S.A., Samuel Minott, 1732—1803, *Boston, Mass.*
533		U.S.A., Sibley and Marble, 1801—1806, *New Haven, Conn.*
534		U.S.A., Simon Sexnine, 1722, *New York, N.Y.*
535		VIENNA (A), 1774—1776, *items of sub-standard purity*
536		STEGE (DK), c. 1750
537		STELLA (I), 15th—16th centuries
538		SULMONA (I), since 13th century, *the stamp changes shape*
539		SUHL (DDR), 17th—18th centuries
540		U.S.A., Samuel Williamson, 1794, *Philadelphia, Pa.*

541		BORDEAUX (F), 1687—1691, *charge*
542		PRAGUE (CS), 1776—1806, *for sub-standard purity*
543		TOULOUSE (F), 1774—1780, *charge — minor items*
544		ST GERMAIN (F), 1781, *charge — medium-sized items*
545		ST GERMAIN (F), 1781, *charge — large items*

LETTER T

546		TORGAU (DDR), 16th—17th centuries
547		TAMPERE (SF), up to 1943
548		PARIS (F), "maison commune" for 1735
549		PARIS (F), "maison commune" for 1782

550		NANTES (F), 1744, *charge*
551		TOURNAI (Doornijk) (B), 1st half of 17th century
552		SALINS (F), 1779
553		TOURNAI (Doornijk) (B), 2nd half of 18th century
554		TOURNAI (Doornijk) (B), 2nd half of 18th century
555		TOURS (F), 1780—1789, *charge — minor items*
556		U.S.A., Timothy Bontecou Jr., 1723—1789, *New Haven, Conn.*
557		U.S.A., Trott and Brooks, 1798, *New London, Conn.*
558		U.S.A., Thomas Carson, 1815, *Albany, N.Y.*
559		U.S.A., Timothy Dwight, 1645—1691, *Boston, Mass.*

560		FORMER AUSTRO-HUNGARIAN EMPIRE, 1810—1824, *tax mark for smaller items (confirmation of payment of special fee)*
561 562		FORMER AUSTRO-HUNGARIAN EMPIRE, 1809—1810, *exemption mark for smaller items (exempt from consignment to State Treasury)*
563		FORMER AUSTRO-HUNGARIAN EMPIRE, 1809—1810, *exemption mark for larger items (exempt from consignment to State Treasury)*
564		FORMER AUSTRO-HUNGARIAN EMPIRE, 1810—1824, *tax mark for larger items (confirmation of payment of special fee) for significance of letter see mark No 1901*
565		ZELENOGORSK (Terijoki) (SU), up to 1943
566		U.S.A., Thomas Knox Emery, 1781—1815, *Boston, Mass.*
567		U.S.A., Thomas Millner, 1690—1745, *Boston, Mass.*
568		TOULOUSE (F), 1780—1789, *charge, minor items*
569		TOLEDO (E), 17th century

570	TOLEDO (E), c. 1600
571	U.S.A., Thomas Skinner, 1712—1761, *New York, N.Y.*
572	U.S.A., Thomas Sparrow, 1764—1784, *Annapolis, Md.*
573	U.S.A., Thomas Townshendt, 1727, *Boston, Mass.*
574	TUNISIA, 1904, *review*
575	U.S.A., Thomas You, 1756, *Charleston, S.C.*

LETTER U

576	UUSIKIRKKO (SF), up to 1943
577	ULRICEHAMN (S), 18th—19th centuries
578	PARIS (F), "maison commune" for 1783

LETTER V

579	PARIS (F), "maison commune" for 1760

580		SENLIS (F), 1747
581		LILLE (F), 1732, *date letter*
582		TROYES (F), 1772, *charge*
583		VIRTON (B), 18th century
584		PARIS (F), "maison commune" for 1655
585		TROYES (F), 1774—1780, *charge?*
586		PARIS (F), "maison commune" for 1736
587		TROYES (F), 1768—1774, *charge*
588		U.S.A., Peter van Dyke, 1684—1750, *New York, N.Y.*
589		U.S.A., Nicholas Roosevelt, 1745—1769, *New York, N.Y.*

590 591		FORMER AUSTRO-HUNGARIAN EMPIRE, 1810—1824, *inventory mark for items manufactured after 1810*
592		KOMÁRNO (CS), KOMÁROM (H), from 17th century to the end of 18th century
593		U.S.A., van Ness and Waterman, 1835, *New York, N.Y.*

LETTER W

594		VIIPURI (SF), up to 1943
595		VISBY (S), 18th century
596		WROCŁAW (PL), 2nd half of 17th century up to c. 1740
597		WEIMAR (DDR), early 17th century
598		VISBY (S), 19th century
599		VÄXJÖ (S), 18th—19th centuries
600		VEVEY (CH), 18th century

601		LILLE (F), 1780—1789, *reconnaissance*
602		VAMMALA (SF), up to 1943
603		VARBERG (S), early 18th century
604		U.S.A., William B. North, 1787—1838, *New York, N.Y.*
605		U.S.A., William Clark, 1774, *New Milford, Conn.*
606		U.S.A., William Cross, 1712, *Boston, Mass.*
607		U.S.A., W. M. Cowel, 1682—1736, *Boston, Mass.*
608		U.S.A., William Paris, 1728—1804, *Annapolis, Md.*
609		U.S.A., William Gale, 1816, *New York, N.Y.*
610		U.S.A., Woodward and Grosjean, 1847, *Boston, Mass.*
611		U.S.A., William Huertin, 1731—1771, *New York, N.Y.*
612		U.S.A., William Homes, 1717—1783, *Boston, Mass.*

613		U.S.A., William Hollingshead, 1770, *Philadelphia, Pa.*
614		U.S.A., Wood and Hughes, 1846, *New York, N.Y.*
615		U.S.A., Benjamin Wynkoop 1675—1751, *New York, N.Y.*
616		U.S.A., William McParlin, 1780—1850, *Maryland*
617		U.S.A., William Rouse, 1639—1705, *Boston, Mass.*
618		U.S.A., Pelletreau and Richards, 1825, *New York, N.Y.*
619		U.S.A., William Vilant, 1725, *Philadelphia, Pa.*
620		U.S.A., William Whetcroft, 1735—1799, *Baltimore, Md.*
621		U.S.A., William Ward, 1742—1828, *Lichtfield, Conn.*
622		U.S.A., W.W. Gaskins, 1830, *Providence, R.I.*

LETTER X

623		PARIS (F), "maison commune" for 1690

624		PARIS (F), "maison commune" for 1714
625		PARIS (F), "maison commune" for 1761
626		PARIS (F), "maison commune" for 1666
627		BESANÇON (F), 1782
628		AMIENS (F), 1774—1780, *charge — large items*
629		AMIENS (F), 1780—1791, *charge — large items*
630		EXETER (GB), 1575—1698, *several variations*
631		PARIS (F), 1691—1698, *contremarque — small items*
632 633 634		BESANÇON (F), first third of 18th century
635 636		BESANÇON (F), 1674—1689

637 638	BESANÇON (F), late 18th century
639	KARLSKRONA (S), 17th—18th centuries
640	BESANÇON (F), 17th century
641 642	AMIENS (F), 1768—1774, *charge — large items*

LETTER Y

643	PARIS (F), "maison commune" for 1692
644	SALINS (F), 1759
645	BOURGES (F), 1780—1789, *charge — large items*
646	BOURGES (F), 1774—1780, *charge — large items*
647	VERSAILLES (F), 1780

648		IEPER (Ypres) (B), 2nd half of 17th century
649		BOURGES (F), 1768—1774, *charge — minor items*
650		IEPER (YPRES) (B), 1701—1713

LETTER Z

651		ZÜRICH (CH), 17th century
652		MANNHEIM (D), 17th—18th centuries
653		ZERBST (D), 18th century, different varieties of shields
654		PARIS (F), "maison commune" for 1763
655		PARIS (F), "maison commune" for 1643
656		BESANÇON (F), 1730

657	BESANÇON (F), 1783
658	PARIS (F), "maison commune" for 1739
659	NORRKÖPING (S), 17th—18th centuries
660	GRENOBLE (F), 1780—1791, *charge — large items*
661	GRENOBLE (F), 1775—1780, *charge — large items*
662	ZÜRICH (CH), 17th—18th centuries
663	GRENOBLE (F), 1756—1762, *charge*
664	ZITTAU (DDR), c. 1750
665	ZÜRICH (CH), 17th—18th centuries
666	U.S.A.,Zachariah Brigden, 1734—1787, *Boston, Mass.*

667		BESANÇON (F), 1730
668		FRANCE, 1809—1819, *import mark for small items*
669		MILAN (I), 1810—1859, *mark of the guarantee office*

NUMERALS

670		BRAGA (P), 1886—1919, *export mark 800/1000*
671		LISBON (P), 1886—1919 *export mark 800/1000*
672 **673**		OPORTO (P), 1886—1919, *export mark 800/1000*
674		OPORTO (P), 1919—1938, *export mark*
675		GONDOMAR (P), 1919—1938, *export mark*
676		LISBON (P), 1919—1938, *export mark*

677		PARIS (F), "maison commune" for 1581
678		TBILISI (Tiflis) (SU), 1830
679		SPAIN, 1881—1934, *purity 750/1000*
680		RENNES (F), 1780—1789, *charge — large items*
681		RENNES (F), 1774—1780, *charge — large items*
682		BESANÇON (F), 18th century?
683		FORMER AUSTRO-HUNGARIAN EMPIRE, 1806—1809, *restamped hallmark for large items; for significance of letter see mark No. 1901, here Prague*
684		TUNISIA, since 1905, *Public Assayer's mark*
685		COLOGNE (D), mid-18th century

686		STRASBOURG (F), 2nd half of 18th century
687		STRASBOURG (F), c. 1650—c. 1750
688		COLOGNE (D), end of 18th century
689		WÜRZBURG (D), 18th century
690		WÜRZBURG (D), 18th century
691		TRIESTE, 18th century
692		MANNHEIM (D), 1737—1766
693		PROVINS (F), 1784—1789
694		JAPAN, since 1928, *mark of purity in thousandths*
695		FINLAND, 1810—1972, *mark of purity in thousandths*

696		SKÄNNINGE (S), 18th—19th centuries
697		TORSHÄLLA (S), 18th century
698		VELIKI USTYUG (SU), 1755—1767
699		VELIKI USTYUG (SU), 1837—1896
700		RYAZAN (SU), 18th and 19th centuries
701		VELIKI USTYUG (SU), 1783—1814
702		KIEV (SU), from 1778 to the beginning of 19th century
703		KIEV (SU), 1848—1865
704		SANTIAGO (E), 16th century

705		BRUSSELS (Bruxelles) (B), 1750—c. 1760
706		ASKERSUND (S), 18th century
707		LIDKÖPING (S), 17th—19th centuries
708		UGLICH (SU), 1762—1778
709		ASKERSUND (S), early 19th century
710		SÖDERTÄLJE (S), 18th—19th centuries
711		MARIEFRED (S), 18th—19th centuries
712		ARCHANGEL (SU), 1763—1768
713		ARCHANGEL (SU), 1796—1798
714		ARCHANGEL (SU), 2nd half of 19th century

715		ARCHANGEL (SU), 1880—1890
716		MUNICH (D), c. 1700
717		MUNICH (D), changing date, here 1752
718		MUNICH (D), with two numerals in the date, 1762—1860, *many* *variations of the shield*
719		GREAT BRITAIN, 1697—1716, *"Britannia"*
720		GREAT BRITAIN, 1716—1717, *"Britannia"*
721		GREAT BRITAIN, 1731—1732, *"Britannia"*
722		GREAT BRITAIN, 1863—1864, *"Britannia"*
723		TORSHÄLLA (S), 19th century
724		NORRKÖPING (S), 18th century

725	VIBORG (DK), 17th—18th centuries
726	BRUSSELS (Bruxelles) (B), early 18th century
727	STOCKHOLM (S), 1600—1700
728	WROCŁAW (PL), from the end of 17th century to 1842, *many variations*
729	WROCŁAW (PL), since 1843, *the numeral changes according to the year*
730	CHARTRES (F), 1768—1774, *contremarque*
731	SENLIS (F), 1784—1789
732	PARIS (F), 1819—1838, *guarantee for medium-sized items*
733	FRANCE — departments, 1798—1809, *guarantee for medium-sized items*
734	FRANCE — departments, 1798—1809, *guarantee for medium-sized items*

735		PARIS (F), 1793—1794 (1840?), *guarantee of the goldsmiths' guild for silver of any purity (also export mark up to 1840?)*
736		PARIS (F), 1798—1809, *guarantee for medium-sized items*
737		PARIS (F), 1798—1809, *guarantee for medium-sized items*
738		YUGOSLAVIA, 1882—1919, *purity 800/1000 — large items, valid on the territory of the former Serbian Kingdom*
739		YUGOSLAVIA, 1882—1919, *purity 750/1000 — large items, valid on the territory of the former Serbian Kingdom*
740		PARIS (F), end of 1794—1797, *guarantee of the goldsmiths' guild for purity 958/1000 (also export mark up to 1840?)*
741		METZ (F), 1774—1780, *décharge — minor items*
742		BLOIS (F), 1768—1774, *décharge*
743		SENS (F), 1768—1774, *décharge*

744		DIJON (F), 1780—1791, *décharge — minor items*
745		FRANCE, 1 September — 31 October 1809, *"general review"*, mark for large items
746		ROUEN (F), 1780—1789, *décharge — minor items*
747		FRANCE, 1798—1809, *import mark for large items*
748		VADSTENA (S), 18th century
749		STOCKHOLM (S), 1720—1740
750		BORDEAUX (F), end of 18th century, *décharge*
751		CAEN (F), 1774—1780, *décharge — large items*
752		BORDEAUX (F), 1774—1780, *décharge — minor items*
753		TROYES (F), 1768—1774, *décharge*

754		PARIS (F), 1781—1789, *décharge — large items*
755		PARIS (F), 1783, *décharge — medium-sized items*
756		PARIS (F), 1781—1789, *décharge — minor items*
757		PARIS (F), 1756—1762, *décharge — large items*
758		FERRARA (I), 17th century
759		POITIERS (F), 1780—1791, *décharge — minor items*
760		ORLÉANS (F), 1780—1791, *décharge — large items*
761		PARIS (F), 1768—1774, *décharge — medium-sized items*
762		PARIS (F), 1781—1789, *décharge — medium-sized items*
763		ORLÉANS (F), 1780—1791, *décharge — minor items*

764 **765**	ORLÉANS (F), 1768—1774, *décharge*
766	LYON (F), 1762—1768, *décharge — large items*
767	AMIENS (F), 1768—1774, *décharge*
768	AMIENS (F), 1774—1780, *décharge — minor items*
769	BRAGA (P), 1886—1911, *for older items or antiques*
770	GONDOMAR (P), 1913—1938, *for older items or antiques*
771	OPORTO (P), 1886—1938, *for older items or antiques*
772	GONDOMAR (P), 1886—1913, *for older items or antiques*
773	LISBON (P), 1886—1938, *for older items or antiques*
774	PARIS (F) 1809—1819, *guarantee for large items*

115

775		FRANCE — departments, 1809—1819, *guarantee for large items*
776		MUNICH (D), 16th—17th centuries
777		PARIS (F), 1819—1838, *guarantee for large items*
778		PARIS (F), 9 November 1797 — August(?) 1798, *review mark for small items*
779		FRANCE, 9 November 1797 — August 1798, *general review — mark for large items*
780		PARIS (F), 1819—1838, *import mark for small items*
781		PARIS (F), 1 September— 31 October 1809, *review mark for large items*
782		FRANCE — departments, 1819—1838, *guarantee for large items, the numeral in the mark indicates the seat of the assay office, here 84 — Auxerre*
783		PARIS (F), 1819—1838, *purity 800/1000*
784		FRANCE — departments, 1819—1838, *purity 800/1000*

785		GREAT BRITAIN, 1784—1786, *duty mark* *(head of King George III)*
786		GREAT BRITAIN, 1837—1889/90, *duty mark* *(head of Queen Victoria)*
787		FRANCE — departments, 1840—1879, *export mark*
788		ITALY, 1873—1935, *purity* *950/1000*
789		ITALY, 1873—1935, *purity* *900/1000*
790		ITALY, 1873—1935, *purity* *800/1000*
791		CZECHOSLOVAKIA, 1921—1928 *purity* *950/1000*
792		CZECHOSLOVAKIA, 1921—1928, *purity* *900/1000*
793		CZECHOSLOVAKIA, 1921—1928, purity *800/1000*
794		CZECHOSLOVAKIA, 1921—1928, *purity* *750/1000, for larger items*

795 796 797	YUGOSLAVIA, since 1933, *for large items: purity 950/1000, purity 900/1000, purity 800/1000*
798	LATVIA, c. 1920—c. 1939
799	LATVIA, c. 1920—c. 1939, *purity 875/1000*
800	LATVIA, c. 1920—c. 1939, *import mark, purity 875/1000*
801 802	RUSSIA, 1896—1908, *purity 875/1000 (84 zolotniks)*
803	STOCKHOLM (S), 1700—1850
804	STOCKHOLM (S), 1700—1850
805	STOCKHOLM (S), 1700—1850
806	FREISING (D), 18th century
807	LIÈGE (Luik) (B), 1693

808		NAPLES (I), 17th—18th centuries, *changing shield*
809		MEAUX (F), 1774—1780, *décharge*
810		COMPIÈGNE (F), 1768—1774, *contremarque*
811		PARIS (F), 1768—1774, *décharge — large items*
812		GREAT BRITAIN, 1786—1820, *duty mark (head of King George III)*
813		GREAT BRITAIN, 1820—1830, *duty mark (head of King George IV)*
814		GREAT BRITAIN, 1830—1837, *duty mark (head of King William IV)*
815		FRANCE — departments, 1809—1819, *guarantee for medium-sized items, the numeral in the mark indicates the seat of the assay office, here 25 — Besançon*
816		PARIS (F), 1819—1830, *import mark for large items*

817

PARIS (F), 9 November 1797—August (?) 1798, *review mark for large items*

818

FRANCE, 9 November 1797—August (?) 1798, *general review for small items*

819

PARIS (F), 1809—1819, *guarantee for medium-sized items*

820

BELGIUM, 1831—1869, *"Garantie" — official test of purity*

821

FRANCE, from 1838 up to the present, *guarantee and purity 950/1000 — for large items*

822

FRANCE, from 1838 up to the present, *guarantee and purity 800/1000 — for large items*

823

PARIS (F), 1819—1838, *purity 950/1000*

824

FRANCE — *departments, 1819—1838, purity 950/1000*

825

TUNISIA, since 1905, *purity 800/1000 — small items*

826
827

828
829

FORMER AUSTRO-
HUNGARIAN EMPIRE,
1 January 1867—1 April
1872, *purity 950/1000,
purity 900/1000, purity
800/1000, purity
750/1000; for significance of
letter stamped next to mark
see marks Nos. 830—833*

830
831

832
833

FORMER AUSTRO-
HUNGARIAN EMPIRE,
1 April 1872—1 May 1922
(on the territory of the
Austrian Republic),
*purity 950/1000,
purity 900/1000,
purity 800/1000,
purity 750/1000*

Key to the Marks
A — Vienna (A)
B — Linz (A)
C — Prague (CS)
D — Brno (CS)
E — Cracow (PL)
F — Lvov (SU)
G — Graz (A)
H — Hall (A) (up to 1872)
H — Bregenz (A) (since
1872)
K — Klagenfurt (A)
L — Ljubljana (YU)
M — Trieste
N — Zadar (YU) (only in
1866—67)
P — Pest (H)
R — Košice (CS)
T — Timișoara (R)
U — Alba Iulia (R)
V — Zagreb (YU)

834
835
836

HUNGARY, 1937—1965,
*for large items:
purity 935/1000,
purity 900/1000,
purity 800/1000*

837		RUSSIA, 1908—1917, *purity 875/1000 (84 zolotniks), for items weighing less than 8.5 g*
838		RUSSIA, 1908—1917, *purity 875/1000 (84 zolotniks), for items weighing more than 8.5 g*
839		RUSSIA, 1908—1917, *imported items*
840		RUSSIA, 1908—1917, *items of sub-standard purity*
841		U.S.S.R., 1921—1958, *purity 875/1000, for items weighing less than 10 g*
842		U.S.S.R., 1927—1958, *for items weighing more than 10 g*
843		U.S.S.R., 1927—1958, *imported items*
844		U.S.S.R., 1927—1958, *items of sub-standard purity (of historical or artistic value)*
845		U.S.S.R., 1927—1958, *for decorative or subsidiary parts of the item*
846		BELGIUM, 1831—1869, *mark of purity*

122

847		LYON (F), 1775—1780, *décharge — large items*
848		TOURS (F), 1780—1789, *décharge — minor items*
849		PARIS (F), 1 September—31 October, 1809, *review mark for medium-sized items*
850		LYON (F), 1762—1768, *older items*
851		LYON (F), 1762—1768, *imported items*
852		FRANCE, 1 September—31 October, 1809, *general review mark for small items*
853		PARIS (F), 1781—1789, *contremarque*
854		PARIS (F), 1 September—31 October, 1809, *review mark for small items*
855		ORLÉANS (F), 1774—1780, *décharge — large items*
856		BOURGES (F), 1774—1780, *décharge — large items*
857		BESANÇON (F), 15th century

858		SCHWÄBISCH HALL (D), 18th century
859		NANTES (F), 1762—1769, *imported items*
860		PARIS (F), 1762—1768, *contremarque*
861		ANTWERP (B), 1627—1628
862		ANTWERP (B), 1574—1575
863		ALTENBURG (DDR), 17th century
864		VOLOGDA (SU), 1751
865		VOLOGDA (SU), 1796—1798
866		VOLOGDA (SU), 1843—1850
867		VALK (SU), 1785

868		KIROV(Vyatka) (SU), 18th century
869		SOLIKAMSK (SU), 1736
870		NITRA (CS), *shield changes shape, sometimes the date is given*
871		ESKILSTUNA (S), 18th century
872		JOENSUU (SF), up to 1943
873		ESKILSTUNA (S), 19th century
874		VORONEZH (SU), 1852—1869
875		PARIS — GÉNÉRALITÉ (F), (revenue district), 1775—1781, *imported items*
876		RIOM (F), 1774—1780 *décharge — large items*
877		GRENOBLE (F), 1775—1780, *décharge — large items*

878		BAYONNE (F), 1774—1780, *décharge — minor items*
879		TOURS (F), 1774—1780, *décharge — large items*
880		VILNIUS(Vilna) (SU), 1861
881		FILIPSTAD (S), 1st half of 19th century
882		MOSCOW (SU), 1741—1775, *different variations*
883		MOSCOW (SU), 1780
884		MOSCOW (SU), 1800—1804
885		POLOTSK (SU), 1842—1858
886		TBILISI (Tiflis) (SU), 1847—1861
887		SKÄNNINGE (S), 19th century

MAMMALS

888   YSTAD (S), 18th—19th centuries

889   GRAZ (A), 17th century up to 1717

890   SCHWÄBISCH-GMÜND (D), c. 1762—1786

891   KAZAN (SU), 2nd half of 18th century and 1st half of 19th century

892   KAZAN (SU), 1742

893   KAZAN (SU), 1880—1890, *numeral indicates purity*

894   FLORENCE (I), 16th(?) century

895   FRANCE — departments, 1838—1879, *import mark for silver watches*

896   KAZAN (SU), 1864

897   SWEDEN, ÖSTERGÖTLAND PROVINCE, 18th century

898		VENICE (I), 17th—18th centuries
899		VENICE (I), 16th—18th centuries
900		YUGOSLAVIA, import mark valid from 1882 to 1919 on the territory of the former Serbian Kingdom
901		SCHWÄBISCH-GMÜND (D), early to mid-19th century, *changing shield*
902		BIBERACH a. RISS (D), 18th—19th centuries
903		BIBERACH a. RISS (D), 18th—19th centuries
904		ENGLAND, 1544—1550, *lion passant*
905		ENGLAND, 1550—1558, *lion passant*
906		ENGLAND, 1558—1679, *lion passant*
907		ENGLAND, 1679—1697 and 1719—1739, *lion passant*
908		GREAT BRITAIN, 1739—1756, *lion passant*

909		GREAT BRITAIN, 1756—1822, *lion passant*
910		GREAT BRITAIN, 1822—1896, *lion passant*
911		GREAT BRITAIN, 1822—1896, *lion passant*
912		HEIDELBERG (D), 17th—18th centuries, *various shields*
913		BRUNSWICK (D), 17th—18th centuries, *various shields*
914		DARMSTADT (D), 18th—19th centuries
915		HANNOVER-NEUSTADT (D), 17th—18th centuries
916		WEIMAR (DDR), late 17th century
917		DIJON (F), mid-18th century, *décharge*
918		BAUSKA (SU), 18th century
919		PASSAU (D), 18th century

920	INGOLSTADT (D), 18th century
921	LÜNEBURG (D), 16th—17th centuries, *many variations in different shields*
922	ESTONIA, c. 1920—c. 1939
923	BOLOGNA (I), 18th century
924	KALMAR (S), 17th—18th centuries
925	LYON (F), 1762—1768, *décharge — small items*
926	NORWAY, since 1893, *purity 925—830/1000*
927	LUCCA (I), 17th century
928	VITRÉ (F), 1756—1762, *charge*
929 930	HOLLAND, 1814—1953, *purity 934/1000, purity 833/1000*
931	MORAT (CH), late 18th century

932		VLADIMIR (SU), 1763—1778
933		VLADIMIR (SU), 1857—1863
934		VLADIMIR (SU), 19th century
935		PSKOV (SU), 19th century
936		DÜSSELDORF (D), 18th century
937		KALMAR (S), end of 18th century and 19th century
938		JÖNKÖPING (S), 18th—19th centuries
939		SAULGAU (D), 1707
940		KARLSHAMN (S), 18th—19th centuries
941		KARLOVY VARY (CS), 17th—18th centuries

942		ORADEA (R), *shield changes shape, sometimes with date*
943		FLORENCE (I), 17th—18th centuries
944		BRUSSELS (Bruxelles) (B), early 18th century
945		BRUSSELS (Bruxelles) (B), 1750—*c.* 1760
946		LIÈGE (Luik) (B), 1764—1771
947		LIÈGE (Luik) (B), 1784—1792
948		PARMA (I), 17th century
949		PRAGUE (CS), 1776—1793, *13 lot silver, changing date in the mark*
950		PRAGUE (CS), 1776—1793, *13 lot silver, changing date in the mark*
951		PRAGUE (CS), 1793—1806, *13 lot silver, changing date in the mark*

952		PREŠOV (CS), 1st half of 19th century, *changing date and changing shape of the shield*
953		GRAZ (A), 1718—1775
954		GRAZ (A), 1775—1799
955		GRAZ (A), 1800—1806
956		KLAGENFURT (A), 1775—1806
957		NAMUR (Namen) (B), 16th—17th centuries, *sometimes the date changes in the mark*
958		ZWEIBRÜCKEN (D), 18th century
959		RIBE (DK), 18th—19th centuries
960		DÜSSELDORF (D), 18th century
961		SARAGOSSA (E), 16th century

962		YORK (GB), 1700—1857, *several variations*
963		LINKÖPING (S), 18th century
964		LINKÖPING (S), 19th century
965		AMIENS (F), 1762—1774, *décharge — large items*
966		AMIENS (F), 1774—1780, *décharge — large items*
967		ENGLAND, up to c. 1470, *Leopard's head*
968		ENGLAND, 1470—1515, *Leopard's head, many variations*
969		ENGLAND, 16th—17th centuries, *Leopard's head, many variations*
970		ENGLAND, 1681—1689, *Leopard's head, many variations*
971		GREAT BRITAIN, 1719—1740, *Leopard's head, many variations*

972		GREAT BRITAIN, 1756—1821, *Leopard's head, many variations*
973		GREAT BRITAIN, 1822—1836, *Leopard's head, many variations*
974		GREAT BRITAIN, 1836—1896, *Leopard's head, many variations*
975		GREAT BRITAIN, 1710—1711, *lion's head erased*
976		GREAT BRITAIN, 1717—1718, *lion's head erased*
977		GREAT BRITAIN, 1726—1727, *lion's head erased*
978		GREAT BRITAIN, 1725—1731, *lion's head erased*
979		GREAT BRITAIN, 1863—1864, *lion's head erased*
980		BRUGES (B), c. 1660
981		LYON (F), 1780—1791, *décharge — minor items*

982		FORMER AUSTRO-HUNGARIAN EMPIRE, 1 January, 1867— 1 April, 1872; *for very small items of 750/1000 purity. For significance of letter stamped next to mark, see marks Nos. 830—833*
983		FORMER AUSTRO-HUNGARIAN EMPIRE, 1 April, 1872—1 May, 1922 (on the territory of the Austrian Republic), *for very small items of 750/1000 purity. For significance of letter in the mark see marks Nos. 830—833*
984		STUTTGART (D), 18th—19th centuries, sometimes the mark contains a letter
985		PARIS (F), 1732—1738, *décharge — large and medium-sized items*
986		HANNOVER (D), 18th century, *court silversmiths*
987		WOLFENBÜTTEL (D), 17th—18th century
988		DEBRECEN (H), 1st half of 19th century
989		HORSENS (DK), 18th century
990		BRANIEWO (Braunsberg) (PL), c. 1740

991		PERTH (GB), 1679—1710, *several variations*
992		LIMOGES (F), 1780—1791, *décharge — large items*
993		YUGOSLAVIA, 1919—1933, *imported items, purity 800/1000*
994		YUGOSLAVIA, 1882—1919, *for small items of 800/1000 purity, valid on the territory of the Serbian Kingdom*
995		PARIS (F), 1794—1797, *guarantee of the goldsmiths' guild for purity 843/1000(?) (also import mark up to 1840?)*
996		PARIS (F), 1797, purity 843/1000
997		TOULOUSE (F), 1768—1774, *décharge*
998		LYON (F), 1775—1780, *décharge — minor items*
999		VERSAILLES (F), 1762, *décharge — large items*
1000		CAEN (F), 1780—1791, *décharge — large items*

1001		PAU (F), late 18th century
1002		PAU (F), 1784—1791
1003		FRANCE — Division Centre, 1819—1838, *guarantee for small items*
1004		MARIESTAD (S), 18th—19th centuries
1005		BOURGES (F), 1774—1780 *décharge — minor items*
1006		MARIESTAD (S), 18th century
1007		PARIS (F), 1738—1744, *décharge — large items*
1008		PARIS (F), 1775—1781, *décharge — large items*
1009		LA ROCHELLE (F), 1774—1780, *décharge — small items*
1010		RENNES (F), 1780—1789, *décharge — minor items*

1011		WISMAR (DDR), from the end of 17th century to the beginning of 19th century, *many variations of the shield*
1012		SWITZERLAND, 1882—1892, *purity 875/1000*
1013 **1014**		SWITZERLAND, 1893—1934, *purity 875/1000, larger items, smaller items*
1015		BERLIN, 1st half of 18th century
1016		BERLIN, 2nd half of 18th century, *letter in the mark changes*
1017		YAROSLAVL (SU), 2nd quarter of 18th century
1018		YAROSLAVL (SU), 2nd half of 18th century
1019		YAROSLAVL (SU), 1771—1806
1020		MADRID (E), 18th century
1021		BAMBERG (D), 18th—19th centuries

1022		NOVGOROD (SU), 1764—1846
1023		BERN (CH), 16th century
1024		BERN (CH), 16th century
1025		BERN (CH), 16th century
1026		BERN (CH), c. 1800
1027		GORKI (Nizhni Novgorod) (SU), 1778—1800
1028		ALINGSÅS (S), late 18th century and early 19th century
1029		PARIS (F), 1768—1774, *items for export*
1030		ROSTOV (Yaroslavski) (SU), 1761
1031		GIENGEN (D), 18th century
1032		CHUR (CH), 16th—18th centuries

1033		VARBERG (S), 18th—19th centuries
1034		GORKI (Nizhni Novgorod) (SU), 1859
1035		ST GERMAIN (F), 1732, *charge*
1036		FORMER FRENCH EAST AFRICA, since 1939, *purity 950/1000; changing letter in the mark*
1037		FORMER FRENCH EAST AFRICA, since 1939, *purity 800/1000; changing letter in the mark*
1038		RHODESIA, present-day mark
1039		NANTES (F), 1746, *décharge*
1040		NANTES (F), 1769—1784, *décharge*
1041		ÖSTERSUND (S), 19th century
1042		COMPIÈGNE (F), 1784—1789

1043	PITEÅ (S), 2nd half of 18th century and 19th century
1044	PARIS (F), 1750—1756, *larger older items*
1045	SAUMUR (F), 1756—1762, *décharge*
1046	UMEÅ (S), 2nd half of 18th century and 19th century
1047	STUTTGART (D), 19th century
1048	ELGAVA (Mitava) (SU), 17th century
1049	PARIS (F), 1768—1774, *larger older items*
1050	TUTTLINGEN (D), *c.* 1660
1051	CZECHOSLOVAKIA, 1921—1928, *purity 750/1000; for smaller items*
1052	YUGOSLAVIA, 1919—1933, *purity 800/1000; for small items*
1053	CAEN (F), 1780—1791, *décharge, minor items*

1054		TOURS (F), 1753, *décharge*
1055		POITIERS (F), 1774—1780, *décharge, minor items*
1056		SCHAFFHAUSEN (CH), 16th century
1057		SCHAFFHAUSEN (CH), 17th—18th centuries
1058		HUDIKSVALL (S), 18th century
1059		HUDIKSVALL (S), 18th—19th centuries
1060		METZ (F), 1774—1780, *décharge, large items*
1061		AMIENS (F), 1780—1790, *décharge, minor items*
1062		PARIS (F), 1819—1838, *guarantee for smaller items*
1063		ORLÉANS (F), 1774—1780, *décharge, minor items*
1064		FRANCE, general review from 10 May to 1 October, 1838; *for large items*
1065		LYON (F), 1768—1775, *décharge, small items*

1066		PONTOISE (F), 1768—1774, *contremarque*
1067		PARIS (F), *contremarque décharge, large items*
1068		LA ROCHELLE (F), 1780—1791, *décharge, minor items*
1069		PARIS (F), 1775—1781 *décharge, small items*
1070		CZECHOSLOVAKIA, 1921—1928, purity 900/1000, for smaller items
1071		LIMOGES (F), 1780—1781, *décharge, minor items*
1072		MONTARGIS (F), 1768—1774, *décharge*
1073		ROUEN (F), 1698, *décharge*
1074		SALINS (F), 1784—1789
1075		WINTERTHUR (CH), 18th century
1076		SAUMUR (F), 18th century, *charge*
1077		CAEN (F), 1744—1750, *décharge, minor items*

1078		PARIS (F), 1744—1750, *décharge, large items*
1079		CAEN (F), 1744—1750, *décharge, large items*
1080		ST GERMAIN (F), 1781, *décharge, medium-sized items*
1081		PARIS (F), 1738—1744, *décharge, minor items*
1082		PARIS (F), 1732—1738, *décharge, minor items*
1083		PARIS (F), 1762—1768, *décharge, minor items*
1084		ANGERS (F), 1747, *décharge*
1085		TOURS (F), 1768—1774, *décharge*
1086		CZECHOSLOVAKIA, 1921—1928, *purity 800/1000, for smaller items*
1087		HUNGARY, 1937—1965, *purity 935/1000, for small items*
1088		HUNGARY, 1937—1965, *purity 800/1000, for small items*
1089		PARIS-GÉNÉRALITÉ (revenue district) (F), 1775—1781, *items for export*

1090		PARIS-GÉNÉRALITÉ (revenue district) (F), *1775—1781, older items*
1091		FRANCE, general review from 16 August to 16 November, 1819, *for large items, the numeral in the mark indicates the seat of the Assay Office, here 57—department Nord, Lille*
1092		FORMER AUSTRO-HUNGARIAN EMPIRE, 1 January, 1867—1 April, 1872, purity 800/1000, *for very small items*
1093		FORMER AUSTRO-HUNGARIAN EMPIRE, 1 March, 1872—1 May, 1922 (on the territory of the Austrian Republic) *purity 800/1000 for very small items*
1094		PARIS (F), 1797, *purity 950/1000*
1095		FRANCE, general review from 10 May to 1 October, 1838, *for very small items*
1096		POITIERS (F), 1774—1780, *décharge, large items*
1097 1098		MEAUX (F) 1784—1789
1099		TOURS (F), 1774—1780, *décharge, minor items*
1100		ST GERMAIN, (F) 1732, *décharge*

1101		LA CHARITÉ (F), 1768—1774, *décharge*
1102		TROYES (F) 1768—1774, *décharge*
1103		SWIDNICA (Schweidnitz) (PL) 17th—18th centuries
1104 **1105**		LISBON (P), 1886—1938, *purity 916/1000, purity 833/1000, for large items; tolerance 005/1000*
1106 **1107**		OPORTO (P), 1886—1938, *purity 916/1000, purity 833/1000; for large items; tolerance 005/1000*
1108 **1109**		GONDOMAR (P), 1886—1913, *purity 916/1000, purity 833/1000; for large items; tolerance 005/1000*
1110 **1111**		BRAGA (P), 1886—1911, *purity 916/1000, purity 833/1000; for large items; tolerance 005/1000*
1112 **1113**		GONDOMAR (P), 1913—1938, *purity 916/1000, purity 833/1000; for large items; tolerance 005/1000*
1114 **1115**		LISBON (P), 1886—1938, *purity 916/1000, purity 833/1000; for small items; tolerance 005/1000*
1116 **1117**		OPORTO (P), 1886—1938, *purity 916/1000, purity 833/1000; for small items; tolerance 005/1000*

1118 1119	GONDOMAR (P), 1886—1913, *purity 916/1000, purity 833/1000; for small items; tolerance 005/1000*
1120 1121	BRAGA (P), 1886—1911, *purity 916/1000; purity 833/1000; for small items; tolerance 005/1000*
1122 1123	GONDOMAR (P), 1913—1938, *purity 916/1000, purity 833/1000; for small items; tolerance 005/1000*
1124	YUGOSLAVIA, 1919—1933, *purity 750/1000, for large items*
1125	PARIS (F), 1750—1756, *décharge, large items*
1126	BORDEAUX (F), 1744—1750, *décharge*
1127	PARIS (F), guarantee since 1838; *for small items*
1128	TOULOUSE (F), 1780—1789, *décharge, large items*
1129	PARIS (F), 1768—1774, *medium-sized older items*
1130	RIOM (F), 1780—1789, *décharge, minor items*

1131		IRKUTSK (SU), 1777—1789
1132		TOBOLSK (SU), 1765—1780
1133		IRKUTSK (SU), 1815—1825
1134		UFA (SU), mid-19th century
1135		KRISTIINA (SF), up to 1943
1136		PARIS (F), 1697—1703, *décharge, large items*
1137		WESEL (D), 16th—17th centuries; *sometimes together with date letters*
1138		LA ROCHELLE (F), 1774—1780, *décharge, large items*
1139		ST GERMAIN (F), 1784—1789
1140		JIHLAVA (CS), 1769—1806?, *changing date in the mark*

1141 1142	PARMA and PIACENZA (I), 1818—1872, *purity 917/1000, purity 792/1000; for smaller items*
1143 1144	PARMA and PIACENZA (I), 1818—1872, *purity 917/1000, purity 792/1000*
1145	DONAUWÖRTH (D), 16th—17th centuries
1146	LIÈGE (Luik) (B), mid-16th century
1147	LIÈGE (Luik) (B), 1650—1688
1148	LIÈGE (Luik) (B), 1688—1693
1149	LIÈGE (Luik) (B), 1693—1705?
1150	LIÈGE (Luik) (B), 1693
1151	LIÈGE (Luik) (B), 1711—1723

1152		LIÈGE (Luik) (B), 1724—1743
1153		LIÈGE (Luik) (B), 1744—1763
1154		LIÈGE (Luik) (B), 1764—1771
1155		LIÈGE (Luik) (B), 1772—1784
1156		LIÈGE (Luik) (B), 1784—1792
1157		NOVGOROD (SU), 1717—1732
1158		TULA (SU), 1794
1159		VELIKI USTYUG (SU), 1768—1782
1160		GALICIA (SU), 1769
1161		KALUGA (SU), 1772—1786

1162		KAMENETS-PODOLSK (SU), 1758—1764
1163		MOSCOW (SU), 1712; *many variations*
1164		MOSCOW (SU), 1675—1676; *many variations*
1165		MOSCOW (SU), 1700—1710; *many variations*
1166		MOSCOW (SU), 1740; *many variations*
1167		MOSCOW (SU), 1731; *many variations*
1168		LÜBECK (D), 16th—18th centuries; *many variations*
1169		LENINGRAD (St Petersburg) (SU), 1730—1737; *many variations*
1170		PERTH (GB), up to 1750 (1856?); *various deviations*
1171		MIDDELBURG (NL), 18th century

152

1172		BOLSWARD (NL), 18th century
1173		TRIESTE, 18th century
1174		MINSK (SU), 1871
1175		ÜBERLINGEN (D), 16th—17th centuries
1176		BRNO (CS), from mid-17th century to 1768
1177		BRNO (CS), 1769—1806?; *changing date in the mark*
1178		ZNOJMO (CS), 1769—1806?; *changing date in the mark*
1179		OLOMOUC (CS), 1769—1806?; *changing date in the mark*
1180		MECHELEN (B), 18th century
1181 1182		LISBON (P), 1886—1938; *purity 916/1000, purity 833/1000, for large items; tolerance 002/1000*

1183 1184		**OPORTO (P), 1886—1938,** *purity 916/1000, purity 833/1000, for large items; tolerance 002/1000*
1185 1186		**GONDOMAR (P),** 1886—1913, *purity 916/1000, purity 833/1000, for large items; tolerance 002/1000*
1187 1188		**BRAGA (P), 1886—1911,** *purity 916/1000, purity 833/1000, for large items; tolerance 002/1000*
1189 1190		**GONDOMAR (P),** 1913—1938, *purity 916/1000, purity 833/1000, for large items; tolerance 002/1000*
1191		**SCHWEINFURT (D),** 17th century; *several variations*
1192		**ÜBERLINGEN (D),** 18th century
1193		**AACHEN (D),** from 1573 to the beginning of 19th century; *sometimes with date letter*
1194		**FRANKFURT a.M. (D),** 16th century — mid-18th century; *different variations in stamps*
1195		**U.S.A., Isaiah Wagster,** 1776—1793; *Baltimore, Md.*
1196		**MODENA (I), 1818—1872,** *purity 10 oncie 10/12*

1197	MODENA (I), 1818—1872, *purity 11 oncie 11/12*
1198	MODENA (I), 17th century
1199	TURIN (I), c. 1750
1200	PRUSSIA, tax mark for items manufactured after 25 April, 1809; from 10 September, 1809 onwards for church items exempt from tax (Gratisstempel)
1201	PALERMO (I), 17th century
1202	FRANKFURT a.M. (D), mid-18th century
1203	NEUCHÂTEL (CH), 17th—18th centuries
1204	ARAD (R), early 19th century
1205	ARAD (R), 1847
1206	POTSDAM (DDR), 18th century

1207		OLOMOUC (CS), prior to 1769; *changing date in the mark*
1208		ARBOGA (S), 17th—18th centuries
1209		ARBOGA (S), 17th—18th centuries
1210		ÖREBRO (S), 17th—18th centuries
1211		CHERNIGOV (SU), 1st half of 19th century
1212		MEMMINGEN (D), 16th—17th centuries; *different variations in shields*
1213		RACIBÓRZ (Ratibor) (PL), 17th century
1214		BYTOM (PL), 1736—1770
1215		KAUFBEUREN (D), 18th century
1216		GENEVA (CH), 18th century

1217		PREŠOV (CS), 18th century
1218		WERTHEIM (D), c. 1660
1219		HILDESHEIM (D), 16th—17th centuries
1220		CHEB (CS), 17th—18th centuries
1221		ORENBURG (SU), mid-19th century
1222		SUZDAL (SU), mid-18th century
1223		PARIS (F), 1713—1717, *décharge*
1224		FRANCE, 1798—1809, *purity 950/1000*
1225		FRANCE, 1798—1809, *purity 800/1000*
1226		PARIS (F), 1809—1819, *purity 950/1000*

1227		PARIS (F), 1809—1819, *purity 800/1000*
1228		FRANCE — departments, 1809—1819, purity 950/1000
1229		FRANCE — departments, 1809—1819, purity 800/1000
1230 1231 1232		YUGOSLAVIA, since 1933, *purity 950/1000, purity 900/1000, purity 800/1000, for small items*
1233		TONGEREN (Tongres) (B), c. 1759
1234		ZWICKAU (DDR), 16th—17th centuries
1235 1236 1237		PARIS (F), 1727—1732, *décharge, medium-sized items*
1238		PAU (F), mid-18th century
1239		TOULOUSE (F), 1755, *décharge*
1240		's GRAVENHAGE (NL), 18th century

1241		ROUEN (F), 1768—1774, *décharge*
1242		TOULOUSE (F), 1774—1780, *décharge, minor items*
1243		TOURS (F), late 17th century, *décharge*
1244		PARIS-GÉNÉRALITÉ (revenue district) (F), 1756—1762, *décharge, large items*
1245		BEAUVAIS (F), 1768—1774, *décharge*
1246		KÄKISALMI (SF), up to 1943
1247		PARIS (F), 1704—1712, *contremarque, minor items*
1248		PARIS (F), 1722—1727, *décharge, minor items*
1249		EINSIEDELN (CH), 17th—18th centuries
1250		EINSIEDELN (CH), 18th century
1251		CHARTRES (F), 1784—1789

1252		YUGOSLAVIA, since 1933, *import mark for purity 800/1000*
1253		OPORTO (P), 1886—1938, *special items*
1254		LISBON (P), 1886—1938, *special items*
1255		BRAGA (P), 1886—1911, GONDOMAR (P), 1913—1938, *special items*
1256		VERSAILLES (F), 1768—1774, *décharge, large items*
1257		PARIS-GÉNÉRALITÉ (revenue district) (F), 1756—1762, *décharge, large items*
1258		GRENOBLE (F), 1770, *contremarque*
1259		PARIS-GÉNÉRALITÉ (revenue district) (F), 1768—1774, *décharge, large items*
1260		TOULOUSE (F), 1762—1768, *décharge*
1261		FALKENBERG (S), 18th—19th centuries
1262		FRANKFURT a.d.ODER (DDR), 17th—18th centuries

1263 1264		SWITZERLAND, 1893—1934, *purity 800/1000; larger items, smaller items*
1265		SWITZERLAND, 1882—1892, *purity 800/1000*
1266 1267		LISBON (P), 1886—1938, *purity 916/1000, purity 833/1000, for small items; tolerance 002/1000*
1268 1269		OPORTO (P), 1886—1938, *purity 916/1000, purity 833/1000, for small items, tolerance 002/1000*
1270 1271		GONDOMAR (P), 1886—1913, *purity 916/1000, purity 833/1000, for small items; tolerance 002/1000*
1272 1273		BRAGA (P), 1886—1911, *purity 916/1000, purity 833/1000, tolerance 002/10000*
1274 1275		GONDOMAR (P), 1913—1938, *purity 916/1000, purity 833/1000, for small items; tolerance 002/1000*
1276		FRANCE, general review from 1 September to 31 October, 1809; *for medium-sized items*
1277		PARIS (F), 1781—1789, *imported items*
1278		PARIS (F), 1783, *décharge, medium-sized items*
1279		PARIS (F), 1798, *purity 800/1000*

1280 1281		PARIS (F), 1798, *purity 950/1000, purity 900/1000*
1282		TOULOUSE (F), *décharge, minor items*
1283		PARIS (F), 1744—1750, *décharge, minor items*
1284		PARIS (F), 1783, *décharge, small items*
1285		YUGOSLAVIA, 1882—1919, *purity 750/1000, for small items; valid on the territory of the former Serbian Kingdom*
1286		GRENOBLE (F), 1770, *contremarque*
1287		PARIS-GÉNÉRALITÉ (revenue district) (F), 1768—1774, *décharge, minor items*
1288		PARIS (F), 1750—1766, *décharge, small items*
1289		SAUMUR (F), 1756—1762, *charge*
1290		HUNGARY, 1937—1965, *purity 900/1000, small items*
1291		MALMÖ (S), 17th—19th centuries
1292		MALMÖ (S), 17th—19th centuries

1293		SZCZECIN (Stettin) (PL), 18th century
1294		BEAUMONT-SUR-OISE (F), 1768—1774, *décharge*
1295		FREIBURG i.B. (D), 17th—18th centuries
1296		PARIS (F), 1717—1722, *contremarque, large items*
1297		CHÂTEAU GONTIER (F), 18th century
1298		YUGOSLAVIA, 1919—1933, *purity 750/1000, small items*
1299		CHARTRES (F), 1768—1774, *décharge*
1300		LYON (F), 1768—1755, *contremarque*
1301		ETAMPES (F), 1768—1774, *contremarque*
1302		PONTOISE (F), 1768—1774, *décharge*

1303   FRANCE — DIVISION NORD-EST, 1819—1838, *guarantee for small items*

1304   FRANCE — DIVISION SUD-OUEST, 1819—1838, *guarantee for small items*

1305   PARIS (F), 1738—1744, *contremarque*

1306   MELUN (F), 1784—1789

1307   LAHOLM (S), 18th—19th centuries

1308   MARSTRAND (S), 18th—19th centuries

1309   ÖSTHAMMAR (S), 18th—19th centuries

1310   SIMRISHAMN (S), 19th century

1311   NARVA (SU), 17th century

1312	NARVA (SU), 18th century
1313	ENGELHOLM (S), 18th—19th centuries
1314	UUSIKAUPUNKI (SF), up to 1943
1315	SARATOV (SU), 2nd half of 18th century—19th century
1316	ENKHUISEN (NL), 18th century
1317 **1318** **1319**	RUMANIA, 1906—1920?, *purity 950/1000,* *purity 800/1000,* *purity 750/1000*
1320	FRANCE — DIVISION SUD, 1819—1938, *guarantee for small items*
1321	FRANCE — DIVISION NORD-OUEST, 1819—1838, *guarantee for small items*
1322	BEAUVAIS (F), 1784—1789, *décharge*
1323	TOURS (F), early 18th century, *décharge*
1324	SIMRISHAMN (S), 18th century

1325		ST GERMAIN (F), 1756, *décharge*
1326		PARIS (F), 1744—1750, *older large items*
1327		RENNES (F), 1740, *charge*
1328		NANTES (F), 1731, *décharge*
1329		PARIS (F), 1783, *contremarque*
1330		BRAY-SUR-SEINE (F), 1768—1774, *décharge*
1331		TOULOUSE (F), 17th century, *décharge*
1332		LYON (F), 1768—1775, *imported items*
1333		PARIS (F), 1756—1762, *décharge, minor items*
1334		BORDEAUX (F), 1780—1789, *décharge, minor items*

1335		FRANCE — DIVISION EST, 1819—1838, *guarantee for small items*
1336		PARIS (F), 1768—1774, *import mark for small items*
1337		PROVINS (F), 1768—1774, *décharge*
1338		ETAMPES (F), 1784—1789
1339		FRANCE, 1838—1893, *guarantee for silver watches*
1340		FRANCE, 1838 up to the present, *"petit" guarantee for small items*
1341		LYON (F), 1768—1775, *décharge, large items*
1342		PARIS (F), 1762—1768, *décharge, large items*
1343		FRANCE — DIVISION OUEST, 1819—1838, *guarantee for small items*
1344		ROUEN (F), 1768—1774, *décharge*
1345		ETAMPES (F), 1768—1774, *décharge*

1346	FRANCE, 1838—1864, *import mark*
1347	LISBON (P), since 1891, *for watches of 800/1000 purity*
1348	OPORTO (P), since 1891, *for watches of 800/1000 purity*
1349	LISBON (P), since 1891, *plaqué*
1350	OPORTO (P), since 1891, *plaqué*
1351	FRANCE — DIVISION SUD-EST, 1819—1838, *guarantee for small items*
1352	FONTAINEBLEAU (F), 1768—1774, *contremarque*
1353	CZECHOSLOVAKIA, 1921, *inventory mark*
1354	COULOMMIERS (F), 1768—1774, *contremarque*
1355	GIEN (F), 1768—1774, *décharge*
1356	COMPIÈGNE (F), 1768—1774, *décharge*

1357	METZ (F), 1780—1791, *décharge, small items*
1358	PARIS (F), 1722—1727, *contremarque*
1359	FRANCE — DIVISION NORD, 1819—1838, *guarantee for small items*

PLANTS

1360	EKSJÖ (S), 18th—19th centuries
1361	VIMMERBY (S), 18th—19th centuries
1362	STAVANGER (N), 1st half of 18th century
1363	LINDESBERG (S), 18th century
1364	HEDEMORA (S), late 18th century and 19th century
1365	SWEDEN, BLENKINGEN PROVINCE, 18th century
1366	SWEDEN, BLENKINGEN PROVINCE, 18th century

1367		GLASGOW (GB), from 17th century up to the present, *several variations; rectangular stamp since 1781*
1368		's HERTOGENBOSCH (NL), 17th century
1369		TRIESTE, 1797—1806, for 15 lot silver
1370		TRIESTE, 1797—1806, for 13 lot silver
1371		HOLBAEK (DK), 19th century
1372		UDDEVALLA (S), 18th—19th centuries
1373		PENZA (SU), 1854
1374		NORA (S), late 18th century and 19th century
1375		NORA (S), 18th century
1376		FRANCE-departments, 1819—1838, *import mark for small items*

1377		PERONNE (F), 1768—1774, *imported items*
1378		TOULOUSE (F), 1774—1780, *décharge*
1379		TROYES (F), 1780—1789
1380		PARIS (F), 1756—1762, *contremarque*
1381		PARIS (F), 1762—1768, *charge, minor items*
1382		PARIS (F), 1704—1712, *reconnaissance, minor items*
1383		SENS (F), 1768—1774, *contremarque*
1384		VERSAILLES (F), 1768—1774, *charge, medium-sized items*
1385		RIOM (F), 1780—1789, *décharge, large items*
1386		LYON (F), 1762—1768, *older items*

1387		ROUEN (F), 1780—1789, *décharge, large items*
1388		MANTES (F), 1774—1780, *contremarque*
1389		DIJON (F), 1780—1791, *décharge, large items*
1390 1391		TUNISIA, since 1905, *purity 900/1000, purity 800/1000, large items*
1392		ITALY, 1810—1872, *purity 950/1000, for small items*
1393		ST GERMAIN (F), 1781, *décharge, large items*
1394		PARIS-GÉNÉRALITÉ (revenue district) (F), 1775—1781, *for very small items*
1395		ROUEN (F), 1774—1780, *décharge, minor items*
1396		DIJON (F), 1775—1780, *décharge, large items*
1397		AMIENS (F), 1780—1791, *décharge, large items*

1398		AUGSBURG (D), 1675—1685
1399		AUGSBURG (D), 1680—1696
1400		AUGSBURG (D), 1712—1713
1401		AUGSBURG (D), 1723—1735
1402		AUGSBURG (D), 1723—1735
1403		AUGSBURG (D), *changing letters indicate different periods, here 1787—1789*
1404		RAPPERSWIL (CH), 16th—17th centuries
1405		RAPPERSWIL (CH), 18th century
1406		LANDSKRONA (S), 17th—18th centuries
1407		LANDSKRONA (S), 19th century

1408		FALUN (S), 18th—19th centuries
1409		BORDEAUX (F), late 18th century, *décharge*
1410		VERSAILLES (F), 1780—1789, *décharge, large items*
1411		PARIS (F), review from 16 August to 16 November, 1819; *for large items*
1412		MANTES (F), 1774—1780, *décharge*
1413		GRENOBLE (F), 1780—1791, *décharge, minor items*
1414		SWEDEN, BLENKINGEN PROVINCE, 18th century
1415		PROVINS (F), 1784—1789
1416		FRANCE-departments, 1819—1838, import mark for large items
1417		MELUN (F), 1774—1780, *décharge*

1418		PARIS (F), 1768—1774, *charge, small items*
1419		PARIS (F), 1717—1722, *reconnaissance*
1420		LYON (F), 1768—1775, *older items*
1421		DREUX (F), 1768—1774, *décharge*
1422		LYON (F), 1780—1791, *décharge, large items*
1423		BAYONNE (F), 1780—1789, *décharge, minor items*
1424		DORDRECHT (NL), 18th century
1425		PARIS (F), 1781—1789, *very small items*
1426		PARIS (F), review from 16 August to 16 November, 1819; *for very small items*
1427		ROSENHEIM (D), mid-17th century

1428		TOULOUSE (F), 16th—17th centuries, *décharge*
1429		NORWICH (GB), 1581—1697; *several variations*
1430		PARIS (F), 1756—1762, *reconnaissance*
1431		BAYONNE (F), 1780—1789, *décharge, large items*
1432		BORDEAUX (F), late 18th century, *décharge*
1433		BORDEAUX (F), late 18th century, *décharge*
1434		LYON (F), 1768—1775, *older items*
1435		BORDEAUX (F), late 18th century, *décharge*
1436		GRENOBLE (F), 1780—1791, *décharge, large items*
1437		ST GERMAIN, 1768—1774, *charge, minor items*

1438		TRONDHEIM (N), changing date in the mark
1439		HANNOVER-ALTSTADT (D), 17th—18th centuries; in 17th century two numerals in the mark indicating year
1440		PARIS (F), 1704—1712, *reconnaissance, large items*
1441		BRAȘOV (R), mid-18th century
1442		PARIS (F), 1783, *décharge, very small items*
1443		KIEL (D), 18th century
1444		KIEL (D), 17th century; *changing shield*
1445		PARMA and PIACENZA (I), 1818—1872, *very small items*
1446		PARIS (F), 1684—1687, *very small items*
1447		DIJON (F), 1762—1768, *décharge*

1448		NYSA(Neisse) (PL), 17th—18th centuries; *several varieties of shields; sometimes the mark contains the date*
1449		KOŠICE (CS), from 16th century to c. 1812
1450		ODENSE (DK), 18th century
1451		JÖNKÖPING (S), 17th—18th centuries
1452		ENKÖPING (S), 18th—19th centuries
1453		DILLINGEN a.d. DONAU (D), 1st half of 18th century
1454		PARIS (F), 1680—1684, *décharge, small items*
1455		GRÄNNA (S), 18th—19th centuries
1456		PARIS (F), 1717—1722, *décharge, large items*
1457		ANGERS (F), 1734—1741, *décharge*

1458		PARIS (F), 1717—1722, *décharge, medium-sized items*
1459		LILLE (F), 1750
1460		LILLE (F), 1755
1461		LILLE (F), 1776
1462		LILLE (F), 1732
1463		PARIS (F), 1717—1722, *contremarque, small items*
1464		PARIS (F), 1717—1722, *décharge, large items*
1465		TOULOUSE (F), 16th—17th centuries, *décharge*
1466		TOULOUSE (F), 1726, *décharge*
1467		TOULOUSE (F), 1768—1774, *décharge*

1468		VERSAILLES (F), 1784
1469		CZECHOSLOVAKIA, 1921—1940, *imported items*
1470		PARIS (F), 1677—1680, *charge, large items*
1471		PARIS (F), 1680—1684, *charge; this mark was added to other marks in 1681*
1472		PARIS (F), 1727—1732, *décharge, large items*
1473		YORK (GB), 1562—1700; *several variations*
1474		LINCOLN (GB), c. 1624 and during the period 1640—1650
1475		HALMSTAD (S), 18th—19th centuries
1476		GRENOBLE (F), 1768—1774, *imported items*
1477		RENNES (F), 1774—1780, *décharge, large items*

1478		FALUN (S), 18th—19th centuries
1479		KHARKOV (SU), mid-19th century
1480		GŁOGÓWEK (Ober-Glogau) (PL), 18th century
1481		LYON (F), 1762—1768, *imported items*
1482		VERSAILLES (F), 1780—1789, *décharge, medium-sized items*

CELESTIAL BODIES

1483		PARIS (F), 1722—1727, *décharge, large items*
1484		KUOPIO (SE), up to 1943
1485		FÜRTH (D), 19th century
1486		VARKAUS (SF), up to 1943
1487		YUGOSLAVIA, 1919—1933, *purity 900/1000; larger items*

1488	TURKEY, 1939—1942, *purity 900/1000*
1489	TURKEY, 1939—1942, *purity 800/1000*
1490	TURKEY, 1923—1928, *purity 900/1000*
1491	TURKEY, 1923—1928, *purity 800/1000*
1492	LÜNEBURG (D), *since the beginning of 19th century*
1493	FORMER AUSTRO-HUNGARIAN EMPIRE, 1806—1809, *restamped hallmark for larger items; for. significance of letter in the mark see mark No. 84; here indicating Prague*
1494	FÜRTH (D), 18th century
1495	GERMANY, since 1888, *minimum purity 800/1000*
1496	HALLE a.d. SAALE (DDR), 17th—18th centuries; *changing shields*
1497	MAASTRICHT (NL), 18th century

182

1498		TUNISIA, 1856—1905, *Public Assayer's mark*
1499		PARIS (F), 1684—1687, *reconnaissance*
1500		SPAIN, since 1934, *purity 915/1000*
1501		ROUEN (F), 1768—1774, *décharge*
1502		SPAIN, since 1934, *purity 750/1000*
1503		BRAGA (P), 1881—1887, *minimum purity 750/1000*
1504		GUIMARÃES (P), 1881—1887, *minimum purity 750/1000*
1505		NORDEN (D), 19th century
1506		NORDEN (D), 18th—19th centuries
1507		BOLZANO (I), 18th century

1508		BOLZANO (I), mid-18th century
1509		BOLZANO (I), early 18th century
1510		THUN (CH), 17th century
1511		SION (CH), 17th century
1512		SION (CH), 18th century
1513		DOKKUM (NL), 18th century
1514		HAARLEM (NL), 18th century
1515		GOUDA (NL), 17th century
1516		SÖDERKÖPING (S), 18th—19th centuries
1517		ITALY, 1810—1872, *purity 800/1000, for large items*

1518		ÅMÅL (S), 18th—19th centuries
1519		LEUTKIRCH (D), 17th century
1520		NYKÖPING (S), 17th—19th centuries; *many variations*
1521		EDINBURGH (GB), 16th—17th centuries; *many variations*
1522		SPEIER (D), 17th century
1523		BERGEN (N), 18th—19th centuries; *changing shields*
1524		ST GERMAIN (F), 1768—1774, *contremarque*
1525		TOULOUSE (F), 1750—1756, *charge*
1526		TOURS (F), 1780—1789, *décharge, large items*
1527		ORLÉANS (F), 1762, *décharge*

1528		ALKMAAR (NL), 18th century
1529		NORWICH (GB), *1565—1697; several variations*
1530		TOROPETS (SU), 1802
1531		HANKO (SF), up to 1943
1532		KÖSZEG (H), 1st half of 19th century
1533		BUDAPEST-PEST (H), up to the end of 18th century
1534		BUDAPEST-PEST (H), from c. 1810 to 1865; *changing date*
1535		TIMIȘOARA (R), in different shields and with changing date
1536		NOYON (F), 1768—1774
1537		PRAGUE-NOVÉ MĚSTO (CS), 1562—1776; *changing date*

1538		MAGDEBURG (DDR), 17th century and early 18th century; *more variations*
1539		UHERSKÉ HRADIŠTĚ (CS), early 17th century
1540		RIGA (SU), 19th century
1541		NEWCASTLE (GB), since 1672
1542		DENMARK, since 1893; *control mark, minimum standard purity 830/1000*
1543		HÄLSINGBORG (S), 19th century
1544		NOVI SAD (YU), since the end of 18th century
1545		FALKÖPING (S), 18th—19th centuries
1546		HÄLSINGBORG (S), 1st half of 18th century
1547		EXETER (GB), 1701 — 2nd half of 19th century; *various deviations*

1548		LUND (S), 18th—19th centuries
1549		LUND (S), 18th century
1550		AALBORG (DK), *sometimes with date in the mark*
1551		HÄLSINGBORG (S), late 18th century
1552		NYKÖPING (S), 17th—19th centuries; *many variations*
1553		ZHITOMIR (SU), 1823
1554		MALBORK(Marienburg) (PL), 17th—18th centuries
1555		SOPRON (H), up to 1780s
1556		JÖNKÖPING (S), 18th—19th centuries
1557		BRATISLAVA (CS), up to 1730s

188

1558		ZABKÓWICE ŚLĄSKIE (Frankenstein) (PL), early 18th century
1559		GENOA (I), 17th—18th centuries
1560		TOURNAI (Doornijk) (B), 1st half of 17th century
1561		BAUTZEN (DDR), 18th century
1562		PRAGUE-STARÉ MĚSTO (CS), 1562—1776; *changing date*
1563		BOLESŁAWIEC(Bunzlau) (PL), c. 1750
1564		CRACOW (PL), 1809—1835
1565		ALTONA (D), 18th century; *changing date letters in the mark*
1566		HAMBURG (D), 17th—18th centuries; *from mid-17th century onwards date letters change in the mark*
1567		KOMÁRNO (CS) KOMÁROM (H) 1st half of 19th century

1568		BUDAPEST-BUDA (H), up to the end of 18th century
1569		WEILHEIM (D), 17th—18th centuries
1570		COPENHAGEN (DK), since 1608; *changing date in the mark*
1571		BRATISLAVA (CS), from 1730s to 1860s
1572		SOPRON (H), up to mid-19th century; *changing date*
1573		BUDAPEST-BUDA (H), from c. 1810 to 1865; *changing date*
1574		LEÓN (E), 18th century
1575		CRACOW (PL), 1835—1866, *changing date, here 1845*
1576		SKARA (S), 18th—19th centuries
1577		KALUNDBORG (DK), 17th century

1578		PRAGUE-MALÁ STRANA (CS), 1666—1776; *changing date in the mark*
1579		ESZTERGOM (H), early 19th century
1580		OREL (SU), 1766
1581		CORK (Corcaigh) (EIR), 17th—18th centuries; *different varieties*
1582		KUNGÄLV (S), late 18th century
1583		KLAJPEDA (Memel) (SU), 18th century
1584		CRACOW (PL), 1809—1835
1585		CLUJ (R), from late 18th century to mid-19th century
1586		BANSKÁ ŠTIAVNICA (CS), 1st half of 19th century
1587		ALBA IULIA (R), c. 1850

1588	UHERSKÉ HRADIŠTĚ (CS), 1769—1806?; *changing date*
1589	FRIBOURG (CH), c. 1630
1590	FRIBOURG (CH), c. 1710
1591	MIKULOV (CS), 1769—1806?; *changing date*

OBJECTS

1592	PARIS (F), 1677—1680, *charge, large items*
1593	PARIS (F), 1691—1698, *décharge*
1594	STOCKHOLM (S), 1500—1600
1595	STOCKHOLM (S), 1500—1600
1596	BRAȘOV (R), mid-19th century
1597	FINLAND, since 1810, *control mark for domestic items*

1598	FINLAND, since 1810, *control mark for imported items*
1599 **1600** **1601**	RUMANIA, 1937—1949; *purity 950/1000, purity 800/1000, purity 750/1000*
1602 **1603** **1604**	RUMANIA, up to 1937; *purity 950/1000, purity 800/1000, purity 750/1000*
1605	PARIS (F), 1775—1781; *duty-free items*
1606	PARIS (F), 1697—1703, *décharge, large items*
1607	PARIS (F), 1687—1691, *décharge, large items*
1608	PARIS (F), 1680—1684, *extra mark added in 1681*
1609	PARIS (F), 1680—1684, *décharge, large items*
1610	PARIS (F), 1677—1680, *charge, large items*
1611	BORDEAUX (F), 1687—1691, *décharge*
1612	SIGTUNA (S), 18th century

1613		YUGOSLAVIA, 1919—1933, *imported items of 750/1000 purity*
1614		PARIS (F), 1768—1774, *duty-free items*
1615		SHEFFIELD (GB), from 1773 up to the present; *several variations*
1616 1617		PARIS (F), 1684—1687, *décharge*
1618		BORDEAUX (F), 1774—1780, *décharge*
1619		FRANCE, 1809—1819, *import mark for large items*
1620		OPORTO (P), 1886—1911, *silver rods*
1621		BRAGA (P), 1886—1911, *silver rods*
1622		KALININ (Tver) (SU), 1816—1830
1623		KALININ (Tver) (SU), 19th century; *changing date*

1624		KALUGA (SU), 1864
1625		KALUGA (SU), 1870—1880
1626		KOBLENZ (D), 18th century
1627		SWEDEN, state control mark used from 1752 up to the present
1628		HULL (GB), 1621—1706
1629		BAKU (SU), last quarter of 19th century; *the numeral in the mark indicates purity*
1630		SENLIS (F), 1768—1774, *décharge, medium-sized items*
1631		ELLWANGEN a.d. JAGST (D), 18th century
1632		GHENT (B), 18th century
1633		PARIS (F), 1744—1750, *small older items*

1634		TOURS (F), 18th century, *décharge?*
1635		LANDSHUT (D), mid-18th century
1636		LANDSHUT (D), late 18th century
1637		GRENOBLE (F), 1775—1780, *décharge, minor items*
1638		LA ROCHELLE (F), 1780—1791, *décharge, large items*
1639		PARIS (F), 1768—1774, *imported large items*
1640		PARIS (F), 1781—1789, *Mont de Piété*
1641		MELUN (F), 1774—1780, *contremarque*
1642		DIJON (F), 1774—1780, *décharge, minor items*
1643		LIMOGES (F), 1774—1780, *décharge, minor items*
1644		RIOM (F), 1774—1780, *décharge, small items*

1645		BOURGES (F), 1780—1789, *décharge, minor items*
1646		LYON (F), 1768—1775, *imported items*
1647		VERSAILLES (F), 1762, *décharge, minor items*
1648		AUDENARDE (Oudenaarde) (B), c. 1600
1649		AUDENARDE (Oudenaarde) (B), since 1655
1650		MONTEREAU (F), 1768—1774, *décharge*
1651		RENNES (F), 1774—1780, *décharge, minor items*
1652		VESOUL (F), 1784—1789
1653		BEAUVAIS (F), 1768—1774
1654		ROUEN (F), 1768—1774, *décharge*
1655		METZ (F), 1780—1791, *décharge, large items*

1656	ABBEVILLE (F), 1768—1774
1657	PARIS-GÉNÉRALITÉ (revenue district) (F), 1775—1781, *contremarque*
1658	BASEL (CH), mid-17th century
1659	BASEL (CH), 18th century
1660	BASEL (CH), 17th—18th centuries
1661	BASEL (CH), 18th century
1662	NIVELLES (B), 17th century
1663	EGER (H), 1st half of 19th century
1664	LUDWIGSBURG (D), 19th century
1665 **1666**	ITALY, since 1935, *purity 925/1000*, purity *800/1000*

1667		JAPAN, since 1928; *always with a mark of purity in thousandths*
1668		BELGIUM, 1831—1869, *guarantee for official test of purity*
1669		ESSEN (D), 17th century
1670		ASTRAKHAN (SU), 2nd half of 18th century
1671		ASTRAKHAN (SU), 1st half of 19th century
1672		KEŽMAROK (CS), from early 18th century to c. 1800
1673		KEŽMAROK (CS), c. 1850
1674		HEINOLA (SF), up to 1943
1675		FREIBERG (DDR), 18th—19th centuries
1676		LEIPZIG (DDR), 17th—18th centuries; *changing shields*

1677		DRESDEN (DDR), late 18th century and 19th century
1678		SIBIU (R), since the end of 18th century
1679		TOBOLSK (SU), 1792—1794
1680		ST GERMAIN (F), 1768—1774, *décharge, minor items*
1681		SENLIS (F), 1768—1774, *contremarque*
1682		FRANCE, 1798—1809, *"poinçon de vieux" for older items put on sale again*
1683		FRANCE-departments, 1809—1819, *"petite garantie"*
1684		PARIS (F), 1809—1819, *guarantee for small items*
1685		FRANCE, 1798—1809, *guarantee for small items*
1686		PARIS (F), 1722—1727, *décharge, medium-sized items*

1687	ST GERMAIN (F), 1768—1774, *décharge, large items*
1688	BORDEAUX (F), 1780—1789, *décharge, large items*
1689	SENS (F), 1784—1789
1690	YUGOSLAVIA, 1919—1933, *purity 900/1000;* for small items
1691	UPPSALA (S), 17th—19th centuries
1692	UPPSALA (S), 17th—19th centuries
1693	SÄTER (S), 19th century
1694	JÁCHYMOV (CS), 17th—18th centuries
1695	BANSKÁ ŠTIAVNICA (CS), 17th—18th centuries
1696	SALA (S), 17th—19th centuries

1697		YUGOSLAVIA, 1919—1933. *purity 800/1000, for large items*
1698		BIEL (Bienne) (CH), 18th century
1699		SENLIS (F), 1768—1774, *charge, large items*
1700		BARDEJOV (CS), 18th century
1701		SPIŠSKÁ NOVÁ VES (CS), c. mid-19th century
1702		SORTAVALA (SF), up to 1943
1703		SUNDSVALL (S), 18th—19th centuries
1704		LULEÅ (S), 18th century
1705		LEUVEN (Louvain) (B), 18th century
1706		COULOMMIERS (F), 1768—1774, *décharge*

1707		PÄRNU (SU), 18th century
1708		BREMEN (D), 1st half of 18th century
1709		WORMS (D), turn of 17th and 18th century
1710		BREMEN (D), c. 1750
1711		STANS (CH), 18th century
1712		PLZEŇ (Pilsen) (CS), 18th century
1713		LEGNICA (Liegnitz) (PL), 17th—18th centuries
1714		NEUVILLE (CH), 17th century
1715		RIGA (SU), 16th—18th centuries
1716		LEIDEN (NL), 18th century

1717		REGENSBURG (D), 18th century; *without letter G in 16th and 17th centuries*
1718		LULEÅ (S), 19th century
1719		ROME (I), 17th—18th centuries
1720		ROME (I), late 17th century
1721		ROME (I), late 17th century
1722		STADTAMHOF (D), 1767
1723		TARTU (Derpt) (SU), 17th—18th centuries
1724		NAUMBURG a.d. SAALE (DDR), 16th—18th centuries; *many variations in shields*
1725		STRÄNGNÄS (S), 18th—19th centuries
1726		VERSAILLES (F), 1768—1774, *décharge, medium-sized items*

1727	SENLIS (F), 1768—1774, *décharge, large items*
1728	MEAUX (F) 1774—1780, *contremarque*
1729	BOURGES (F), 1780—1789, *décharge, large items*
1730	PARIS (F), 1727—1732, *contremarque*
1731	DUBLIN (Baile Átha Cliath) (EIR), 17th—19th centuries; *many variations*
1732	PARIS (F), 1781—1789, *older items*
1733	BELGIUM, 1831—1869, *state mark of purity*
1734	PROVÍNS (F), 1768—1774, *contremarque*
1735	PARIS (F), 1768—1774, *contremarque*
1736	URACH (D), c. 1700

1737		HOORN (NL), 17th—18th centuries
1738		STRAUBING (D), mid-18th century
1739		VERSAILLES (F), 1768—1774, *imported items*
1740		SMOLENSK (SU), 2nd half of 18th century and 19th century
1741		MAINZ (D), 18th century; *date stamped separately*
1742		KULDIGA (SU), 18th—19th centuries
1743		OSNABRÜCK (D), early 18th century; *several varieties*
1744		MAINZ (D), 1765—1769
1745		TRNAVA (CS), *shield changes shape; sometimes the mark contains the date*
1746		VÄ (S), 16th century

1747		KREMNICA (CS), up to the end of 18th century
1748		KREMNICA (CS), 1st half of 19th century
1749		MAINZ (D), 19th century
1750		ROYE (F), 1768—1774
1751		ROUEN (F), 1768—1774, *décharge*
1752		MONTDIDIER (F), 1768—1774
1753		MONTREUIL (F), 1768—1774
1754		ROUEN (F), 1774—1780, *décharge, large items*
1755		PERONNE (F), 1768—1774
1756		CALAIS (F), 1768—1774, *imported items*

1757		DIJON (F), 1762—1768, *décharge*
1758		LYON (F), 1762—1768, *contremarque*
1759		LIMOGES (F), 1774—1780, *décharge, large items*
1760		VLISSINGEN (NL), 18th century
1761		DUNDEE (GB), 1628—1840, *many variations*
1762		RENNES (F), 1780—1789, *décharge, large items*
1763		PARIS (F), 1781—1789, *export items*
1764		POITIERS (F), 1780—1791, *décharge, large items*
1765		ST QUENTIN (F), 1768—1774
1766		ROUEN (F), 1768—1774, *décharge*

1767		NANTES (F), 1762—1769, *décharge*
1768		UUSIKAARLEPYY (SF), up to 1943
1769		DREUX (F), 1768—1774, *contremarque*
1770		BAYONNE (F), 1774—1780, *décharge, large items*
1771		BORÅS (S), 18th—19th centuries
1772		SCHÄRDING (A), *c.* 1600
1773		LONS-LE-SAUNIER (F), 1784—1789
1774		AUXERRE (F), 1784—1789
1775		BESANÇON (F), 1784—1789
1776		EDINBURGH (GB), from 1760 up to the present; *assayer's mark*
1777		BESANÇON (F), 1784—1789

1778		FONTAINEBLEAU (F), 1768—1774, *décharge*
1779		TROYES (F), 1780—1789
1780		BEAUMONT-SUR-OISE (F), 1768—1774, *contremarque*
1781		CAEN (F), 1774—1780, *décharge, minor items*
1782		PARIS-GÉNÉRALITÉ (revenue district) (F), 1775—1781, *reconnaissance*
1783		CAEN (F), 1744—1750, *décharge, minor items*
1784		VERSAILLES (F), 1768—1774, *contremarque*
1785		VERSAILLES (F), 1745, *charge*
1786		AMIENS (F), 1768—1774, *décharge*
1787		PARIS (F), 1781—1789, *reconnaissance*

1788		PARIS (F), 1732—1738, *contremarque*
1789		PARIS (F), 1727—1732, *décharge, minor items*
1790		CALAIS (F), 1768—1774
1791		MANTUA (I), 17th century
1792		VENICE (I), control mark prior to 1810
1793		MILAN (I), control mark prior to 1810
1794		ITALY, 1810—1872, *purity 800/1000, for small items*
1795		VASTERVIK (S), 18th—19th centuries
1796		HELSINGØR (DK), 1741
1797		STRÖMSTAD (S), 19th century

1798		CORK (Corcaigh) (EIR), 17th—18th centuries; *more variations*
1799		VÄNERSBORG (S), 18th—19th centuries
1800		KOSTROMA (SU), 1769—1813
1801		VASTERVIK (S), 18th—19th centuries
1802		HJO (S), 18th—19th centuries
1803		KRISTINEHAMN (S), 18th—19th centuries
1804		KOSTROMA (SU), 1880—1890; *numeral indicates purity*
1805		ITALY, 1810—1872, *purity 950/1000, for large items*
1806		SÖDERHAMN (S), 18th—19th centuries
1807		HELSINKI (SF), up to 1943
1808		CAEN (F), 1744—1750, *décharge, large items*

1809		BIRMINGHAM (GB), from 1773 to 20th century; *several variations*
1810		DÜSSELDORF (D), 17th—18th centuries
1811		NORRTÄLJE (S), 18th—19th centuries
1812		CZECHOSLOVAKIA, 1921—1940, *export items*
1813		ODESSA (SU), 1848
1814		LENINGRAD (St Petersburg) (SU), 1851
1815		LENINGRAD (St Petersburg) (SU), 1776—1825
1816		LENINGRAD (St Petersburg) (SU), last quarter of 19th century; *numeral indicates purity*

EMBLEMS

1817		KOSTROMA (SU), 1813—1831
1818		OPORTO (P), 1911—1938, *silver rods*

1819		GONDOMAR (P), 1913—1938, *silver rods*
1820		ROTTERDAM (NL), 18th century
1821		SPAIN, 1881—1934, *purity 916/1000*
1822		LIÈGE (Luik) (B), 1724—1743
1823		LISBON (P), 1886—1938, *silver rods*
1824		KUTNÁ HORA (CS), 17th—18th centuries
1825		NOVOCHERKASK (SU), 1847—1880
1826		GALICIA (SU), 1758—1780
1827		TARTU (Derpt) (SU), 1862
1828		TULA (SU), 1796—19th century

1829		CHESTER (GB), 17th century and from 1780 up to the present; *several variations*
1830		FRIBOURG (CH), mid-18th century
1831		KROMĚŘÍŽ (CS), up to 1798
1832		SWITZERLAND, "Poinçon de Notoriété"; *imitation of French 18th-century marks*
1833		TONGEREN (Tongres) (B), c. 1759
1834		PARIS (F), 1756—1762, *charge, minor items*
1835		LIÈGE (Luik) (B), 1688—1693
1836		LIÈGE (Luik) (B), 1650—1688
1837		LIÈGE (Luik) (B), 1693—1705?
1838		LIÈGE (Luik) (B), 1711—1723

1839		LIÈGE (Luik) (B), 1744—1763
1840		DENDERMONDE (Termonde) (B), 18th century
1841		LEUVEN (Louvain) (B), 18th century
1842		MÜNSTER in Westfalen (D), 16th—17th centuries; *changing shields*
1843		ZUG (CH), 18th century
1844		ZOFINGEN (CH), 18th century
1845		BRNO (CS), from mid-16th century to mid-17th century
1846		LAUSANNE (CH), 18th century
1847		KALUGA (SU), end of 18th century and early 19th century
1848		ZUG (CH), 16th—17th centuries

1849		ULM (D), 17th century
1850		ULM (D), 18th century
1851		ULM (D), 17th—18th centuries
1852		INNSBRUCK (A), 1766—1806
1853		KASSEL (D), 18th century
1854		COLOGNE (D), 2nd half of 17th century; *changing letter*
1855		LIÈGE (Luik) (B), 1772—1784
1856		BADEN in Aargau (CH), 16th—17th centuries
1857		BREGENZ (A), c. 1732
1858		PAYERNE (CH), 16th—17th centuries

1859		LUCERNE (CH), 16th century
1860		SWITZERLAND, 17th—18th centuries, *mark for the Lucerne canton*
1861		LUCERNE (CH), 2nd half of 19th century
1862		PFORZHEIM (D), 18th—19th centuries
1863		CHESTER (GB), 1701—1779
1864		HALBERSTADT (DDR), 18th century; *changing shield*
1865		ANSBACH (D), 17th—18th centuries
1866		BADEN-BADEN (D), 18th—19th centuries
1867		ANSBACH (D), 18th century
1868		KARLSRUHE (D), after 1806

1869		SALINS (F), mid-18th century
1870		UTRECHT (NL), 18th century
1871		ALTENBURG (DDR), 17th—18th centuries; *not certain whether Altenburg, perhaps Annaberg (DDR)*
1872		KASSEL (D), 18th—19th centuries; *changing date letter*
1873		NEUCHÂTEL (CH), 1820—1866
1874		HANAU (D), 18th century
1875		HANAU (D), mid-18th century, (Neu-Hanau)
1876		COURTRAI (Kortrijk) (B), from mid-17th century to the end of 18th century
1877		FRANKENTHAL (D), 17th century
1878		WÜRZBURG (D), early 19th century

1879		VIENNA (A) 1790—1866, *for swordmakers' and watchmakers' wares; 13 lot silver only*
1880		VIENNA (A), 1764—1806, *for swordmakers' and watchmakers' wares; 13 lot silver only*
1881		BANSKÁ BYSTRICA (CS), 18th century; *changing date*
1882		BANSKÁ BYSTRICA (CS), 1st half of 19th century; *changing date*
1883		KOŠICE (CS), from c. 1812 to c. 1867; *changing date*
1884		GYÖR (H), from c. 1815 to c. 1860; *changing date*
1885		VIENNA (A), 1691—1737, *changing date; for 13 lot silver*
1886		LINZ (A), 1737(1787?) — 1806; *changing date*
1887		TURIN (I), since 1678; *changing letters in the mark*
1888		ZWOLLE (NL), 18th century

1889		VIENNA (A), prior to 1530
1890		VIENNA (A), 1530—1548
1891		VIENNA (A), 1570—1674
1892		VIENNA (A), 1675—1737; *changing date*
1893		VIENNA (A), 1737—1784, *for 15 lot silver; changing date*
1894		VIENNA (A), 1737—1784, *for 13 lot silver; changing date*
1895		VIENNA (A), 1791—1806, *for 15 lot silver; changing date*
1896		VIENNA (A), 1784—1806, *for 13 lot silver; changing date*
1897 **1898**		**FORMER AUSTRO-HUNGARIAN EMPIRE,** 1806—1866, *for 15 lot silver; changing date; for significance of letters in the marks see marks Nos. 1901—1902*

1899 1900		**FORMER AUSTRO-HUNGARIAN EMPIRE,** 1806—1824, *for 13 lot silver; changing date; for significance of letters in the marks see marks Nos. 1901—1902*
1901 1902		**FORMER AUSTRO-HUNGARIAN EMPIRE,** 1825—1866, *for 13 lot silver; changing date*

Key to the Marks:
A — Vienna (A)
B — Prague (CS)
C — Salzburg (A)
D — Lvov (SU)
E — Cracow (PL) only
    during the 1807—1809
    period;
E — Hall (A), 1824—1866
F — Brno (CS)
G — Linz (A)
H — Graz (A)
I — Klagenfurt (A)
K — Ljubljana (YU)
L — Trieste

1903	CRAILSHEIM (D), 17th century
1904	TÜBINGEN (D), 16th—17th centuries
1905	MONS (Bergen), (B), 18th century
1906	HÄLSINGBORG (S), 19th century
1907	SWITZERLAND, "Poinçon de de Notoriété"; *imitation of French 18th-century marks*
1908	BRZEG (Brieg) (PL), 16th—17th centuries

1909		TOULOUSE (F), 17th century, *charge?*
1910		KROMĚŘÍŽ (CS), 1769—1806; *changing date*
1911		WSCHOWA (Fraustadt) (PL), 17th—18th centuries
1912		SENLIS (F), 1768—1774, *charge, medium-sized items*
1913		MANTES (F), 1784—1789
1914		STRALSUND (DDR), 17th century
1915		KURSK (SU), 19th century
1916		U.S.A., Michael Wilcox, 1772—1799, Maryland
1917		BRAY-SUR-SEINE (F), 1768—1774
1918		TOULOUSE (F), 16th—17th centuries, *décharge*

1919		VERSAILLES (F), 1762, *charge*
1920		BISCHOFSWERDA (DDR), early 18th century
1921		VERSAILLES (F), 1768—1774, *charge, large items*
1922		ST GERMAIN (F), 1768—1774, *charge*
1923		LYON (F), 1768—1775, *charge, small items*
1924		RAUMA (SF), up to 1943
1925		ZUTPHEN (NL), 18th century
1926		PADERBORN (D), 18th century
1927		EUTIN (D), 17th century
1928		FULDA (D), early 18th century

224

1929		TALLINN (Revel) (SU), *c.* 1780
1930		TALLINN (Revel) (SU), 18th century
1931		GYÖR (H), 1st half of 18th century
1932		SÖLVESBORG (S), 19th century
1933		BOULOGNE (F), 1768—1774
1934		LANDSBERG a.d. LECH (D), 17th—18th centuries
1935		GEERAARDSBERGEN (B), c. 1608
1936		ATH (Aeth) (B), 1662—1788, *changing shields*
1937		FRIEDBERG (D), 17th century
1938		KÖPING (S), 18th century

1939		KÖPING (S), c. 1800
1940		KOSTROMA (SU), 1870s; *numeral indicates purity*
1941		CHERSON (SU), last quarter of 19th century; *numeral indicates purity*
1942		SCHWYZ (CH), 17th—18th centuries
1943		ALOST (Aalst) (B), mid-18th century
1944		BADEN in Aargau (CH), 17th—18th centuries
1945		LAVAL (F), 1728
1946		KALININGRAD (Königsberg) (SU), late 17th century up to 1800; *more variations*
1947		TURIN (I), 18th century
1948		KOSTROMA (SU), 1746

1949		KONSTANZ (D), 19th century
1950		ELBLĄG (Elbing) (PL), late 17th century and 18th century
1951		GDAŃSK (Danzig) (PL), 17th—18th centuries
1952		BREDA (NL), 17th century
1953		AMSTERDAM (NL), 18th century
1954		HAMMELBURG (D), early 18th century
1955		PADERBORN (D), 17th century
1956		TÜBINGEN (D), 18th century
1957		TBILISI (Tiflis) (SU), last quarter of 19th century

1958		DEBRECEN (H), 2nd half of 18th century
1959		LEVOČA (CS), from 16th to early 19th century; *shield changes shape*
1960		IEPER (Ypres) (B), 2nd half of 17th century
1961		KONSTANZ (D), 18th century
1962		KONSTANZ (D), late 17th century
1963		LEVOČA (CS), 1st half of 19th century
1964		CZECHOSLOVAKIA, 1929—1940, *purity 950/1000*
1965		CZECHOSLOVAKIA, 1929—1940, *purity 925/1000*
1966		CZECHOSLOVAKIA, 1929—1940, *purity 900/1000*
1967		CZECHOSLOVAKIA, 1929—1940, *purity 835/1000*
1968		CZECHOSLOVAKIA, 1929—1940, *purity 800/1000*

1969		TURKEY, 1923, *purity 900/1000*
1970		TURKEY, 1923, *purity 800/1000*
1971		TUNISIA, 1856—1905, *"Khálés" confirmation*
1972		TUNISIA, 1856—1905, *"Sahha" guarantee*
1973		TUNISIA, 1856—1905, *"Sekka" purity (900/1000)*
1974		TUNIS (TN), 1856—1905, *beys' marks*
1975		TUNIS (TN), 1856—1905, *beys' marks*
1976		TUNIS (TN), 1856—1905, *beys' marks*
1977		TUNIS (TN), 1856—1905, *beys' marks*
1978		DJERBA (TN), 1856—1905

1979		SOUSSE (TN), 1856—1905
1980		SFAX (TN), 1856—1905
1981		GABES (TN), 1856—1905
1982		TURKEY, 1844—1923, *purity 900/1000*
1983 **1984** **1985**		BENI SUEF (ET), since 1916, *purity 900/1000;* *800/1000; 600/1000*
1986 **1987** **1988**		TANTA (ET), since 1916, *purity 900/1000; 800/1000; 600/1000*
1989 **1990** **1991**		CAIRO (ET), since 1916, *purity 900/1000;* *800/1000; 600/1000*
1992 **1993** **1994**	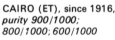	ALEXANDRIA (ET), since 1916, *purity 900/1000;* *800/1000; 600/1000*

INDEX OF CITIES
AND COUNTRIES

The mark numbers are indexed by city. Those marks used throughout the territory of a given country are listed under the name of that country.

632—638, 640, 656, 657, 667,
682, 857, 1775, 1777
Biberach a. d. Riss (D) 902, 903
Biel (Bienne) (CH) 1698
Bienne *see* Biel (CH)
Birmingham (GB) 1809
Bischofswerda (DDR) 1920
Blois (F) 742
Bochnia (PL) 127
Bolesławiec (Bunzlau) (PL) 1563
Bologna (I) 923
Bolsward (NL) 1172
Bolzano (I) 1507—1509
Borås (S) 87, 1771
Bordeaux (F) 99, 125, 310, 315,
316—318, 320—322, 324,
328, 541, 750, 752, 1126, 1334,
1409, 1432, 1433, 1435, 1611,
1618, 1688
Boulogne (F) 1933
Bourges (F) 100, 124, 645, 646,
649, 856, 1005, 1645, 1729
Braniewo (Braunsberg) (PL) 990
Braga (P) 109, 670, 769, 1110,
1111, 1120, 1121, 1187, 1188,
1255, 1272, 1273, 1503, 1621
Braşov (Kronstadt), (Brassó) (R)
1441, 1596
Brassó *see* Braşov (R)
Bratislava (Pressburg), (Pozsony)
(CS) 1557, 1571
Braunsberg *see* Braniewo (PL)
Braunschweig (D) 913
Bray-sur-Seine (F) 1330, 1917
Breda (NL) 1952
Bregenz (A) 79, 80, 826—833,
982, 983, 1857
Bremen (D) 1708, 1710
Breslau *see* Wrocław (PL)
Brevik (N) 119
Brieg *see* Brzeg (PL)
Brno (CS) 79, 80, 84, 826—
833, 982, 983, 1176, 1177,
1845, 1897—1902
Brody (SU) 127
Bruges (Brugge) (B) 86, 980
Brugge *see* Bruges
Brussels (B) 705, 726, 944, 945
Brzeg (Brieg) (PL) 85, 1908
Budapest (H) 458, 1533, 1534,
1568, 1573 *(see also* Pest*)*
Bunzlau *see* Bolesławiec (PL)

Burgos (E) 120
Bytom (PL) 1214

Caen (F) 67, 130, 133, 134, 143,
751, 1000, 1053, 1077, 1079,
1781, 1783, 1808
Cairo (ET) 1989—1991
Calais (F) 1756, 1790
Calatayud (E) 137
Carlsburg *see* Alba Iulia (R)
Castellon de la Plana (E) 138
Cervantes (E) 142
Cervera (E) 142
Chartres (F) 213, 730, 1251,
1299
Chateau-Gontier (F) 1297
Cheb (Eger) (CS) 1220
Chernigov (SU) 1211
Chernovtsy (SU) 127
Chester (GB) 1829, 1863
Chur (CH) 1032
Cluj (Kolozsvár), (Klausenburg)
(R) 1585
Cologne (D) 685, 688, 1854
Compiègne (F) 810, 1042, 1356
Copenhagen (DK) 1570
Corcaigh (Cork) (EIR) 1581, 1798
Córdoba (E) 147
Cork *see* Corcaigh (EIR)
Coulommiers (F) 1354, 1706
Cracow (Kraków) (PL) 79, 80, 84,
826—833, 982, 983, 1564,
1575, 1584, 1897—1900
Crailsheim (D) 1903
Czechoslovakia 290, 791—794,
1051, 1070, 1086, 1353, 1469,
1812, 1964—1968

Danzig *see* Gdańsk (PL)
Darmstadt (D) 914
Debrecen (H) 988, 1958
den Bosch *see* 's Hertogenbosch (NL)
Dendermonde (Termonde) (B) 1840
Denmark 1542
Derpt *see* Tartu (SU)
Dessau (D) 151
Dijon (F) 155, 298, 427, 434—
436, 439, 440, 442, 443, 445,
448, 449, 744, 917, 1389,
1396, 1447, 1642, 1757
Dillingen a. d. Donau (D) 1453
Djerba (TN) 1978

Zagreb (Agram) (YU) 79, 80, 826
—833, 982, 983
Zaleshchiki (SU) 127
Zamość (PL) 127
Zaragoza (E) 961
Zelenogorsk (Terijoki) (SU) 565
Zerbst (D) 653
Zhitomir (SU) 1553
Zholkiev (SU) 127

Zittau (DDR) 664
Znojmo (CS) 1178
Zofingen (CH) 1844
Zug (CH) 1843, 1848
Zürich (CH) 651, 662, 665
Zutfen (NL) 1925
Zweibrücken (D) 958
Zwickau (DDR) 1234
Zwolle (NL) 1888

INDEX OF
AMERICAN MASTERS

Adam, I., 265
Andras & Richard, 74
Andrews, Henry, 250
Anthony, Joseph and Sons, 294
Avery, Samuel, 517

Bailey, Loring, 347
Bancker, Adrien, 61
Bardick, George, 234
Bartholomew Le Roux, 117
Bayley & Douglas, 163
Beach and Ward, 123
Benjamin, John, 266
Besley, Thanvet, 88
Blackman, John Starr, 302
Boehme, Charles L., 146
Boelen, Henricus, 252
Boelen, Jacob, 268
Bontecou, Timothy Jr., 556
Boyce, John, 295
Boyd, Joseph W., 304
Boyer, Daniel, 162
Bradley, Phineas, 456
Brasher, Ephraim, 190
Brevoort, John, 116
Brigden, Zachariah, 666
Brookhouse, Robert, 490
Brower and Rusher, 118
Buel, Abel, 60
Buer, Esekiel, 191
Burrill, Samuel, 522
Burt, John, 267
Burt, Samuel, 521

Camman, Alexander, 65
Candell, Charles, 140
Carman, John, 269

Carson, Thomas, 558
Charters, Cann & Dunn, 141
Chaudrons, Simon & Co., 523
Clark, I., 270
Clark, William, 605
Cleveland & Post, 148
Coddington, John, 273
Cole, Albert, 66
Collins, Arnold, 64
Coney, John, 271, 272
Conyers, Joseph, 491
Cowell, W. M., 607
Crosby, Jonathan, 296
Cross, William, 606

Davenport, Jonathan, 276
David, John, 275
David, Peter, 457
Denise, John, 288
Denise, John, New York, 297
De Parisien, Otto Paul, 420
de Spiegel, Jacobus van, 529
Dixwell, John, 274
Douglas, Robert, 492
Downing & Phelps, 167
Drowne, Shem, 525
Dupuy & Sons, 164
Dwight, Timothy, 559

Edwards, John, 277, 278
Emery, Stephen, 526
Emery, Thomas Knox, 566
Eoff, Edgar M., 194
Eoff & Phyfe, 197

Faris, William, 608
Faulkner, J. W., 305

244